MW00462631

HYPSOCONSCIOUSNESS

TECHNIQUES FOR ACHIEVING PERSONAL SUCCESS

BY
JOHN BAINES

Edited by the Editorial Staff
of the John Baines Institute, Inc.

1995
Published by
John Baines Institute, Inc
P.O. Box 8556 • F.D.R. Station • New York, NY 10150

HypsoConsciousness
(Originally published as
    "Tecnicas de Hipsoconsciencia para el Exito Personal")
    By John Baines
    Translated from Spanish by Josephine Bregazzi
    Copyright 1995 by John Baines
    Cover photography by Jose Luis Sanchis
    Graphic design by Ivette Montes de Oca

ISBN 1-882692-02-0
Library of Congress Catalog Card Number: 94-096631
1st Edition 1995

Published by John Baines Institute, Inc.
Printed in the United States of America

TABLE OF CONTENTS

TO THE READER

Our modern world of rapid social, political, and technological change leaves much to be desired when trying to extract meaning from the kaleidoscope of our day-to-day lives. Behind all the difficulties that we encounter as we move through life driven to find "the answer," one single fundamental fact obliges us to suffer a host of needless ills, sufferings, misunderstandings and disappointments. **This is the fact of man's low level of awareness.**

Because our minds are continually pulled back and forth between future worries of events that have not yet occurred, and past experiences that cannot be changed, we live in a type of semi-sleep, where we are robbed of our very "existence." The unlimited potential of the Human Spirit is stuck firmly in an extremely limited, rigid and programmed mire that binds us through poor education, bad habits, and a society that continually pushes the human being towards excessive haste, short attention spans, instant gratification and an avoidance of the experience of life itself. Unbeknownst to us, we have fallen into a spiritual trap that *moves us faster and faster away from the only place where fundamental reality resides:* **the present moment.**

This book is only a road map, a guidebook that will point you towards a more profound understanding of yourself and the world around you. Everything you will encounter in this book is eminently practical, and the benefits you receive will be in proportion to your honest effort and sincere desire **to get more out of life.**

If the ideas laid out in this book strike a chord in you, and if you earnestly carry out the techniques shared in the coming pages, previously unknown vistas will open up before you. This process of "waking up" is a journey of self-discovery. Once you muster the courage to take the first step forward, you have everything to gain — and nothing to lose except the barriers that stand between you and success, serenity, and a profound understanding of what it means **TO LIVE . . .**

MODERN MAN AND HIS "DISEASE"

The social structure is a well-organized ensemble within which each individual fulfills his role and plays a part. Man's cultural acquisitions have led him to the gradual solution of his problems of subsistence, which in past eras were very harsh. Governing institutions have taken over the management of the life of the group, so that the individual lives his life according to the rules of civilization. To a certain degree, the world seems to be what all believe it should be within the parameters of progress. Modern man feels proud of his civilization, satisfied with his gregarious life, and he considers himself conqueror of the World, without questioning for one instant the veracity of this assumption.

In the course of his continual activity, he rarely considers the long, arduous process implicit in the shaping of the existing cultural heritage. As is well known, "Society" is man's creation, based on his gradual adaptation to Nature. This same adaptation led him to the production of culture, to the forming of certain habits, practices and customs, that is, to the establishment of regular and permanent forms of collective behavior. Custom, tradition, and public opinion are all powerful formative factors of the personality. Due to their peculiar and intangible constitution, these factors strongly influence behavior, character, and the individual's physical and mental development. Through a process of learning, and through the development of his intelligence, man is obliged to adapt to "Society," be governed by its moral and institutional codes and submit to its cultural influence. In order to attain this adaptation, he must employ his intelligence to think, analyze, reflect, understand, and draw certain conclusions, or reach solutions which will then determine personal conduct.

Since a man depends on, lives, and functions in "Society," his adaptation to it is absolutely obligatory, and appears as a compulsive and violating element of his self-determination. Those who do not adapt are alienated from the benefits of community life.

Thus the social organism is granted a quality of virtual omnipotence, bordering on the divine, permitting no chance for error, nor any open disagreement. One cannot conceive of modern man as divorced from the social group. Indeed, it is considered desirable and estimable to conform to patterns of conduct deemed appropriate to our civilization as well as to yearn after a knowledge of its culture.

This structural organization, in which each part affects the whole and is in turn influenced by it, has led the individual to a displacement and projection of his "I." [1] That individual "I" has been absorbed and assimilated by the "great social I." When the individual says "I," he really means "we." This group identification has resulted in a series of highly interesting phenomena, some of them beneficial, others harmful. Among the resulting damages to individual identity, this book will address only those caused by the lack of a reflective, mature, judicious, and adult "I" in the individual.

---

[1] In this book, the "I" in quotation marks, represents the indissoluble unity of the individual's conscious experience, identity and essence. I, without quotation marks, represents the social I, which is that part of the individual that has fallen under the influence of and been absorbed by collective behavior and thought.

Modern man exhibits a notable lack of a reflective "I," merely possessing instead a stereotypical one, which is invariably the result of a social dissociation. When he thinks, this "social-individual I" invariably falls under the compulsive influences of collective conduct and thought, both of which are interwoven into his very essence.

The common denominator of modern man is a lack of self-control in the broadest sense of the word. This lack of self-control means an incapacity to bring the human machine, particularly the brain, to an adequate functioning. It also means an incapacity to fully use one's mental powers; the difficulty in maintaining an adequate state of physical and mental health; discontentment; anguish; disorientation; and a low, nebulous mental state as one's habitual condition.

The individual is the faithful recorder and reflection of local and global collective reactions. He is merely a cog in the enormous, complex social mechanism. Any movement in this machinery immediately influences this tiny cog called man.

Progress, with its ever-growing rhythm, has led man to a perpetual striving after technological, economic, and cultural betterment. Presently, day-to-day living is increasingly volatile and complex. Each instant of each day must be seized in order for one to produce more, and thus be able to keep up a certain social and economic standard of living. The more complex that life becomes, the greater is the collective demand on each individual. For example, there is an increasingly greater requirement for humanistic or university training demanded of the individual who is applying for certain types of work, and the more this training increases, the more rigorous is the selection of the human material. Daily life presents a competition to survive and to attain a high socio-economic standard of living. Thus a sense of haste pervades modern man. He lives too rapidly and thinks too superficially. He is unable to adequately utilize the precious gifts with which he has been endowed. His intelligence is not enough to avert nervous tension, pessimistic ideas, and destructive emotions. His will power is often of no help in conquering bad habits or in controlling his passions. His judgment does not always enable him to see the truth beyond appearances. His faculties do not allow him to free himself from those negative influences which come from the collective emotional and mental state.

There is a collective neurosis of haste, an economic psychosis which obliges the individual to continuously make strenuous efforts to keep up with social demands.

The disease of our time is exaggerated nervous tension, the ramifications of which have not yet been recognized in all their magnitude. Nervous tension is the determining cause of cardiovascular diseases, mental and nervous ailments, and psychosomatic illnesses.

It is a modern disease in as much as it is motivated by factors pertinent to our time. It is motivated by the growing velocity and complexity of life, the disproportionate growth of culture, the accelerated advance of science and technology, the frenetic activity and agglomeration of big cities, the struggle for life, the speed of communications, music and noise, the insecurity about the future of humanity, excessive advertising and indoctrination, and the deficiency in true human communication.

In referring to nervous tension, what is really meant is "exaggerated tension," since "tension" in itself is a normal phenomenon and one necessary to human life. Below are examined in detail the causes which produce tension in order to later be able to prescribe the means by which one can avoid their destructive effects.

The Growing Velocity and Complexity of Life and the Disproportionate Growth of Culture.

On a daily basis, the individual has to face diverse, complex and varying demands. Man lives in a complicated world and has to solve problems every moment of the day. Everything changes too quickly and before the individual manages to adapt completely to a certain situation, it changes and he has to consider a new approach. This complexity and necessity for versatility leads to a basic disorientation. Such a variety of factors often make one lose sight of any points of reference, experiences, ideologies and concepts.

Each day throughout the world, thousands of books are published on the subjects of new techniques and new knowledge. The enormous cultural machinery created by the human being threatens to engulf him, or at least drive him mad. There is no relationship between the velocity of cultural advance and the human capacity for learning. This velocity of change has caused an uncontrollable state of collective anguish and distress.

The Rapid Advance of Science and Technology

Do science and technology advance faster than the human being can bear? Certainly, and this advance may become a serious threat for the future if appropriate measures of control and education are not taken. We know that any technical advance forces the individual to make an effort of adaptation that requires a certain period of time. If the changes are too fast and numerous, then man cannot manage to adapt quickly enough and is left behind. This intense and continuous effort of adaptation may produce distress, neurosis, anguish and other debilitating conditions.

The Activity and Agglomeration of Big Cities; the Struggle for Life; Music and Noise

The individual begins to feel enslaved by the human mass which is in perpetual motion. His daily interactions with others require him to maintain intense competition in order to ascend the social ladder. Collective haste and disarray, endemic to large cities, arouse a similar response in him. The ceaseless roar of machines and vehicles, strident music, the bustle and congestion, the permanent preoccupation with daily living, all keep his nervous system in a state of constant tension.

The Speed of Communications and Insecurity about the Future of Humanity

The press and radio constantly bombard the individual with disconcerting news from all parts of the world. In ancient times, most of the events that took place daily were ignored and communications took months or even years to reach their destination. Unfortunately, today there is an informational atmosphere that is markedly morbid in which basically only those tumultuous events in which there is bloodshed or which are of an alarming nature qualify as "news." This has transformed the mentality of the great mass to such a degree that it seeks precisely the type of morbid information that arouses the imagination and it ignores news of positive events. The natural result of this type of information in the individual, is a subconscious state of anxiety which becomes chronic over time.

Alarming news of wars in certain parts of the world and of the prospects of world war make one live in an inner climate of anxiety. Each individual has the "sword of Damocles" hanging over his head.

The Excess of Advertising and Indoctrination

The individual is continuously and repeatedly bombarded by commercial publicity which infiltrates his privacy and attempts to control his mind, and directs his preferences towards specific goods or services. As these impacts are varied and numerous, they at times create profound conflicts in the subconscious mind and of course bring on a state of tension. Similarly, diverse doctrines, as well as political and religious ideologies attempt to gain followers and submit their minds to constant pressure.

The Lack of Profound Communication Between Human Beings

Social life requires a personal effort of communication that is at times extremely tiring, especially when one is in daily contact with neurotic people. For instance, two people will often argue heatedly on a certain matter, and will never agree or realize that each is stating exactly the same thing, but without managing to communicate it to the other party.

Other factors which hinder communication, apart from varying levels in the command of language between people are cultural differences, prejudices, dogmatism, political and religious convictions, and even personal motives. Finally, it requires a tremendous psychic effort to truly communicate with others, since a person not only has to surmount these obstacles, but is often incapable of acknowledging that such obstacles even exist.

There are many widely known negative conditions that affect modern man as a consequence of nervous tension, which display vague, imprecise, and variable symptoms. Headaches, chronic tiredness, lack of mental concentration, discontentment, anxiety, depressive states, nervousness, worry, and disorientation, are all frequent problems. In these cases one can basically observe an ingrained state of nervous tension, leading to a gradual loss of *"joie de vivre"* and a diminishment of the intellectual faculties. Those are however, only the visible manifestations. There are other more profound, more serious, and far more important conditions that are hard to perceive and identify which are extremely dangerous precisely because of their subtlety. This refers to certain reactions of the subconscious in the face of tension which may lead an individual to a notable diminishing of his intellectual capabilities.

As a result of the factors related to tension listed above, man loses his self-confidence. Only privileged individuals have complete faith in themselves. Usually, the individual seeks the means to join groups where he has no need to take great responsibilities. Other people only trust themselves superficially because they are plagued by an underlying latent state of fear. A feeling of individual security is extremely important because it is the prerequisite for the shaping of a mature and stable personality. Fear and anxiety however, are latent states of the whole of humanity and it is difficult to escape them.

The easiest and most frequent mental approach is that of letting oneself be swept along by the current, of following the dictates of the group, and of seeking the approval of others for one's own initiatives. The individual I that is identified with society adopts as its own all the latent emotional, mental, and instinctive states of the group which he accepts as valid for himself. The processes of observation, reflection and logical reasoning are seriously held back by a passive submission to collective patterns. Unfortunately, the individual does not usually struggle against the tendency to identify completely with his social environment, and instead considers it normal and desirable and believes that therein lies a sort of distinctive sign of intellectuality, sensitivity, civilization and culture.

Through literature, the press and the cinema, what is exalted is violence, morbid sentimentality, fatalism, and the giving of value to nothing. False idols such as money, sex, and muscle, strike the individual from an early age, thereby creating in his mind an erroneous scale of ideal values.

One cannot attain complete self-fulfillment unless one acknowledges and understands that he does not live in a normal world, but rather in a neurotic one; one from which he must escape to a certain extent in order to shape his own personal norms of conduct, as well as ideological and philosophical concepts, which can only be born of mature and serene reflection.

Young people lead particularly disoriented lives, because they have to act in a world that is still to be discovered, not having yet received adequate training to this end. They are obliged to study and accumulate knowledge without having first learned to think. They are obliged to make decisions without having learned to judge and must submit themselves to the mill of the cultural and social machinery imposed upon them. Youthful rebellion is really a quite natural phenomenon that demonstrates an effort to avoid being swallowed up, to shape one's own lifestyle, and to not be forced and compelled to take in prefabricated concepts and rules.

While it is true that tension, anxiety and insecurity have also existed in other eras as well, the whirlwind of life has never spun as fast as today, and the human being has never been submitted to as many and varied simultaneous pressures.

"To be or not to be," the great dilemma of the soul, is the difference between BEING AN INDIVIDUAL AND NOT BEING AN INDIVIDUAL; between being an adult who mentally subsists by his own means, or a child who clings emotionally to "Mother Society."

STRESS

The human being is endowed with a physiological mechanism that enables him to adapt to variations in his surrounding environment and thus maintain internal equilibrium. This mechanism is called *homeostasis*, and is the capacity to maintain organic and psychological stability. Disease is a struggle to maintain the homeostatic equilibrium of tissues. In the face of aggression, the organism immediately reacts to avoid an imbalance. A fever, for example, is the effort of the organism to return to normalcy.

Organic equilibrium can be symbolized as an immobile pendulum. Any stimulus of sufficient intensity will set this pendulum in motion. Stress is the effort to return to the point of equilibrium. Hans

Selye, a Canadian doctor, defines it as follows: "Stress is the state manifested by a specific syndrome, consisting of all the non-specific changes brought about within a biological system. Stress is the common denominator of the reactions of adaptation of the organism."

No one is free from stress, in as much as it is a reaction produced in all living organisms, even in lower species which have no nervous systems. It is a phenomenon indigenous to living beings that confront the environment.

The whole of man's life implies confrontation with the environment. The individual cannot conceive of himself as an isolated entity. The different events of his existence submit him to constant demands for adaptation. If he does not manage to adapt, he seriously harms his health and welfare. The individual lives daily with the continuous effort to adapt, that is, he lives under the influence of stress. This is not necessarily harmful, but instead is an element inherent to the fact of living. Therefore, no one is totally free from stress.

There is thus a type of stress that is compatible with a state of health and another type which is pathological. It is in the pathological sense that the term is used in this chapter.

The elements that provoke a reaction of stress in the individual (medically termed *"general adaptation syndrome."*) are called stress agents. Stress agents can be bacteria, fungi, toxic substances, extreme temperatures or problems of an emotional type. The "general adaptation syndrome" is a determining factor in high blood-pressure, heart and blood vessel diseases, kidney diseases, arthritis, inflammatory skin and eye diseases, allergies, nervous and mental disorders, sexual disorders, digestive ailments, metabolic disorders and cancer.

An individual under the influence of stress (remember the term is used here in its pathological sense) lives in a permanent state of restlessness. Each difficult situation, each problem, each piece of bad news, increases his stock of nervousness. The pressure in his "inner boiler" rises slowly until some trivial event brings on a sudden overflow. The tense individual depletes himself unnecessarily because he squanders nervous energy in huge quantities. A state of tension generally involves a division in the affected individual's personality, since he feels hounded by various demands and cannot decide which to attend to first.

Tension may present itself as a general organic state or as something that manifests itself only through the muscles, the emotions or the mind. We can thus speak of emotional, mental, or muscular tension. However, there is a common factor in all cases of tension, and that is *worry*. It is possible to bring on an artificial neurosis in a laboratory mouse, by "worrying it," that is, by submitting it to a continuous and sustained effort to adapt. Due to this phenomenon, certain people are more predisposed to stress than others. The pessimist, for example, invites a state of artificial stress as a result of his gloomy thoughts, while the optimist acquires a certain resistance to tension. The effects of stress depend on many factors that are also difficult to analyze, such as biological and cultural heritage, the shaping of the personality, one's medical history, temperament, etc.

In order to clarify certain points in the stress mechanism it is essential to know its three stages: 1) *period of alarm;* 2) *period of resistance;* 3) *period of exhaustion.*

The period of alarm is the basic response of the

organism to a stimulus to which it is not adapted. Within this period a stage of shock and another of counter-shock are in turn distinguishable. The stage of shock includes the organic reactions which are produced before the resistance or defense mechanisms kick in. In this phase a series of changes are produced in the endocrinal function, metabolism, composition of the blood, breathing, etc. In the phase of counter-shock, a homeostatic reaction is produced to counter the changes listed above by which the circuit of organic defense is set in motion.

The period of resistance occurs when the organism receives exposure to a stress stimulus that has been experienced before and to which it displays high tolerance. However, when a new and different stress stimulus is produced, the individual slips once more into the first period of alarm.

The period of exhaustion occurs when an organism has been continuously submitted to an alarm stimulus for a long period of time, eventually causing it to lose its resistance.

It can be understood then how adaptation to the diverse stimuli of alarm or stress is produced, since the organism develops resistance and adapts. By the same process a sudden stress or shock may force the organism to evade disease since it activates the defense circuits. In ancient times, the same remedies were applied for different illnesses with positive outcomes and cures in many cases. The witch doctor who frightens the patient with horrifying masks and threats of death, sometimes manages to cure him by unconsciously using the stress principle. Blood-letting, flagellation, and ice-cold baths also act on the same principle. In the case of mental diseases, the administration of artificial shocks is still used today by means of electric currents.

An alarm stimulus, by upsetting the individual's homeostasis, profoundly affects his vital mechanism. Anguish does not discriminate according to the individual's qualities or defects since it attacks the brave, the cowardly, the cautious, and the imprudent alike. The constant repetition of alarm stimuli eventually shapes or transforms a normal personality into an anxious one. Neurosis, nervousness and asthenia are no more than basic forms of anxiety seeking an outlet. There is also, however, a normal anxiety which is produced in the case of danger that is germane to a healthy person.

In many individuals, the stress stimulus may be particularly motivated by psychic conflicts which generally originate from a contradiction between the conscious and instinctive parts of their psyches. The sexual impulse plays an important part in these cases, as well.

Whenever speaking of tension, the strong latent impulse that springs from repressed emotions and impulses, known as repression, should be considered. Emotions that are suppressed for years become as destructive as poison. Some psychiatrists consider repression of the sexual impulse to be the primordial structural cause of neurosis in civilized communities. Any impulse that is restricted increases the pressure of one's "psychic boiler." A fitting example would be that of an individual who is insulted by another to the point that he feels a strong impulse to hit the person insulting him, but his social I or education, prevents him from doing so and he represses the impulse. His gentlemanly behavior has created a latent state of tension within him. The nervous and emotional state aroused by a violent event remains long after the incident is over, not as a conscious state but as a vague uneasiness and anxiety.

The state of tension created as a prelude to

action is well known to all, particularly when it is an action of extreme importance. It is of great interest, for example, to observe the racers in the 100 meter sprint just before they start. They are really living the race before it begins and this imaginative experience burdens them with heavy stress. If for some reason the race were to be cancelled at the last second, a state of tension would have occurred just the same. This illustrates that most tensions are produced by the imaginative anticipation of events that certain people constantly experience. This bad habit causes a huge waste of nervous energy due to the unnecessary worry that it evokes.

There are several degrees of tension. We will basically consider three of them: *worry, anxiety, and anguish.*

Worry is a vague feeling of insecurity and nervousness often becoming chronic and inseparable from everyday life.

Anxiety is a more intense uneasiness due to the pressure of particular events and circumstances.

Anguish is a more violent manifestation when the person feels his own existence threatened. Anguish is fear of death and it mobilizes certain defense mechanisms which cause the affected individual to enter into a sudden nervous and vital "combustion," so to speak.

When faced with the threat of death, the human being's defense mechanisms are set in motion, prodigiously increasing his energy and physiological resistance, so that he is able to carry out great feats of prowess. If this danger is constant and uninterrupted, the individual rapidly reaches a state of exhaustion where his defenses drop abruptly.

It is not possible for a person to constantly keep up his activity without rest, because he periodically needs to free himself from stress to re-establish homeostatic equilibrium. This makes it extremely necessary to conserve one's energy and to sleep nightly in order to compensate for the wearing-down process of stress.

One of the common habitual manifestations of the state of tension is chronic tiredness. Neurotic fatigue is particularly noticeable when awakening from sleep. An individual suffering from asthenia, psychically refuses to get up and prefers to stay in bed. It is difficult and depressing for him to have to do any type of muscular activity. He feels dull and tired. The morning is the time when people prepare to face their daily responsibilities. It is the starting-point for one's daily activity. When the day is over, so are to a certain extent, one's responsibilities and obligations. The individual suffering from asthenia however, begins to feel a state of profound well-being at this time which then goes on till late at night, with the same cycle being repeated the following day. There are often a series of subjective sensations which accompany this condition, such as palpitations, a feeling of pressure in the heart, breathing difficulties, etc. All forms of tension reveal an insufficiency of energy, a state of exhaustion that obliges the organism to over-work itself.

In the average healthy man with a normal constitution, there are two main reasons why he may lack vital energy: excessive waste of it during the day and insufficient recovery of it during sleep. The wasting of this energy always originates in the improper administration of nervous energy caused by bad habits. However strange it may seem, modern education does not teach the development of positive imaginative and emotional habits. We are taught from childhood how to wash daily, how not to overeat, how to observe certain rules of language and social conduct, but the emotions and the imagination are left aside, as if they were not at all important. For example, one of the most pernicious habits is that of wanting to do several things at the same time, which undoubtedly brings on tension and wear and tear. Another bad habit is that of constantly recalling unpleasant events that have already taken place.

Below are listed some illnesses of which stress is the principal cause:

a) Diseases of the heart and blood-vessels such as endocarditis, myocarditis, pericarditis, cardiac neurosis, palpitations, angina pectoris, arteriosclerosis, etc.
b) Kidney diseases.
c) Eclampsia, a major toxemia occurring in pregnancy or during childbirth.
d) Rheumatoid arthritis.
e) Inflammatory skin diseases such as erythema, eczema, rashes, impetigo, psoriasis, hives, itching, diabetes, gout, etc.
f) Allergies.
g) Sexual disorders.

h) Gastric disorders such as gastritis, ulcers, cancer of the stomach and esophagus, irritable bowel syndrome, diarrhea, constipation, etc.

i) Metabolic illnesses such as anemia, scurvy, etc.

j) Cancer.

k) Mental and nervous illnesses such as spasms, neuralgia, cephalgia, migraine headaches, insomnia, neurasthenia, hysteria, psychosis, etc.

l) Obesity.

From this list, if we only consider the harm done by heart diseases and mental and nervous illnesses alone, we can get a good idea of the impact caused by stress. When the pathological manifestations of a state of tension appear, one often resorts to tranquilizers, which act by momentarily freeing the cerebral cortex from perturbing influences. However, these drugs have poisonous effects and cannot be taken indefinitely. Used in excess, they can have harmful effects on the patient's mental and physical state, possibly causing peptic ulcers and ulcerative colitis, for example.

Inexplicably, medical science has not granted the art of relaxation the tremendous importance it has as a natural preventative and cure for states of anxiety.

THE ANGUISHED INDIVIDUAL

Each day, man experiences a series of emotions, sensations, outbursts of anger, aggressions, repressions and frustrations. Emotion is the reaction of the organism to disturbing situations, whether they be pleasant or unpleasant. Emotion has been defined as a "state of agitation," a "disturbance of the equilibrium," and an "intense, random and disorganized reaction to a stimulus." Violent emotion of any type is accompanied by physiological and mental modifications. During an intense emotional state, an abnormal potency of the nervous influx is produced, exceeding normal channels, perturbing and confounding certain faculties of the brain which are thus momentarily annulled. Interesting reactions occur physiologically that indicate that the organism is preparing to fight. Some of the changes are as follows:

dilation of the pupils, an increase in the heart rate, increase in blood pressure, change in the rhythm and depth of breathing with an increase in the consumption of oxygen, increase of sugar in the blood, overworking of the sweat-glands, inhibition of saliva and gastric secretions, and an improvement in the contractive ability of the muscles. An intense emotional state always represents a deviation from normality since the normal state would be a state of calm and equilibrium.

The changes produced by emotion are however useful for those who have to either flee or attack. Emotion raises one's energy to a maximum level and prolongs the amount of time available for useful effort. An individual faced with death can accomplish fantastic physical feats. Emotional states, by temporarily disturbing the equilibrium, set in motion the circuits of organic defense. Homeostasis is the power of the organism to maintain its internal equilibrium and it constantly acts to restore that same equilibrium. During an emotional state, the strength of one's homeostatic ability is severely challenged. It is thus easily understandable that states of emotional tension affect the whole organic mechanism by disrupting these important homeostatic functions.

The most perturbing emotional state is that produced by fear of an imaginary danger or one that is not yet real. This fear manifests itself in the form of anguish.

Freud stated that all anguish is really anguish about death. The individual feels his own existence threatened, not in an immediate or material way, but in a projected and imaginary sense.

Krapf thinks that "the first experiences of anguish in the individual are due to hypoxia of a passing nature that are suffered while the individual is still in the womb and that these first threats to existence create biological memories which once and for all locate the feeling of anguish in the vital mechanism of oxygenation, even though later on the outer world, it does not reduce the supply of oxygen immediately . . . Subjective anxieties are usually accompanied by reflex hypoxia."

Two groups of anguish-causing stimuli can be distinguished: the internal and the external. However, as anguish is a phenomenon that sets the whole individual's personality in motion, the origin of the internal and external stimuli is really centralized on the relationship of man to his environment.

In order to better explain the first cause of anguish, insight into the shaping of the personality and its psychoanalytical structure is pertinent. The personality has been mostly studied as a differentiating factor that marks individuality. Gordon Allport in _The Psychology of the Personality,_ states that "the personality is the product of each one's complex cultural history." However, "no characteristic of the personality is free from hereditary influences. An individual's personality is the means of adaptive or survival adjustment, resulting from the interaction of his organic demands and an environment that is at one and the same time receptive and hostile to these demands, an interaction that takes place by means of a plastic and modifiable nervous system. In the process of adjustment between the organic demands and those of the environment, the central nervous system develops certain characteristic formations which are habits, attitudes, personal traits, forms of sublimation and thought. These characteristic modes of adjustment taken collectively, make up the personality."

The personality is not formed at birth but is gradually shaped by an individual's diverse experiences. "Impulses" play an important part in its formation, being the fundamental motives which originate in the physiology and chemistry of the body. Basic impulses are the result of bodily demands. Hunger, for example, is a result of the lack of food in the body. Impulses require an adjustment in order to satisfy their demand. An impulse is always a state of organic tension that grows in intensity until the organism acts in such a way that relieves the tension thus accumulated.

The vegetative nervous system constantly demands diverse adjustments which are carried out by the cerebro-spinal system. This must constantly exert itself to give the individual comfort and security, because he is trapped between his emotional demands and the limitations and requirements of the environment. This interaction between the vegetative and central systems constantly gives rise to diverse mental conflicts, since all impulses basically seek to acquire or avoid something, that is, the individual desires to obtain something or avoid something that threatens his security. However, in everyday life, what is desirable is often mixed with what is undesirable. A person with a delicate stomach for example, would like to eat rich food, but is afraid of the consequences. This causes a struggle. In more complex situations, the mind sometimes overworks in order to arrive at the right decision.

Perhaps the most important organic demands are the sexual and nutritional ones. The free and natural satisfaction of the sexual impulse is hindered by the dictates of civilization, and the repression of it, is probably the main source of tension in man today.

The environment continually hinders one's desires, threatens one's peace of mind and presents the individual with different problems. Adaptation to various situations, together with the demands of the individual's motives, require an adjustment in order to satisfy all these impulses. To this effect, people acquire different types of habits, that is, adjustment mechanisms that are extraordinarily complex because there are many possible reactions to each single motive. The degree of maturity of the adaptation mechanisms sheds quite a bit of light on the causes of anguish.

The adult possesses certain capacities to make conscious adjustments. On the other hand, the child lacks them. However, the child's impulses, all except for the sexual, are just as strong as those of the adult. In order to adjust, the infant reacts to the internal changes with emotional excitement, with crying, and with reflexive physical activity. Fundamentally, the baby reacts emotionally to his needs with his external reflexes and obtains his parents' attention and care upon which his satisfaction depends.

The adjustment mechanisms of an adult can either be mature or childish. They are mature when the individual manages to live in accordance with reality, adapting perfectly to it and reacting to the environment intelligently and reasonably. Immature adjustments are those produced when the individual reacts in a predominantly emotional manner (like a baby), the emotions prevailing over his intellect. In practice, maturity and childishness do not encompass all of a person's reactions but only certain aspects of them. Thus, an individual may be mature in his family relationships but not so in his social life. Certain situations provoke immature adjustments in balanced people because their personalities fail to develop certain characteristics as they remain at a childish level.

Adaptation and adjustment basically depend upon the course followed by the personality during its growth which goes somewhat hand-in-hand with physiological growth. Certain phenomena associated with the development of the personality are directly related to insecurity, anguish, and reactions to stress.

The shaping of the personality can be compared to the building of a pyramid. The foundation represents the cultural and biological inheritance, and the first level, represents its differentiation. Differentiation consists of a specialization or individualization of the baby's diffuse, primary activities. The motor circuits are formed as barriers that inhibit the total excitement of the nervous system, making them limited systems. Inhibition gradually eliminates unnecessary activity so as to attain greater precision. The child's behavior originates in the disordered responses of the body which then differentiate and shape habits and tendencies.

At a higher stage of development, the integration of the separate units of behavior are united into a broader system. Integration perhaps represents the ultimate mental fulfillment which the individual must reach. Integration also means the cohesion of the different systems. A person who has had a life full of rich and varied experiences will surely have a less integrated personality than an uneducated peasant with few habits and traits. Perhaps it is understandable then why a simple man most often has a more stable and balanced personality than that of an intellectual. The process of integration is of extraordinary importance in a person's ability to adapt, since when reflective power is lacking in this process, the individual becomes stagnated and acts according to stereotyped patterns of behavior. Later on, when we have examined the whole process of the shaping of the personality, we shall return to this point.

There is no consistent integration of the diverse experiences within the personality since many of these experiences are not adequately incorporated because they do not succeed in penetrating the psyche, and they "slide off," to be later forgotten. Thus the experience that is assimilated is far less than a passing, momentary experience. This is due to the fact that by nature man does not bother to reflect in order to properly understand new concepts or experiences, but prefers to confront them with his previously formed habits and traits. The mind is stratified with certain forms of thought and the individual considers that it is too difficult and laborious to modify his own integration. Of course, this phenomenon alone causes difficulties in adaptation, since the world is constantly changing, obliging the individual to renew his psychic posture. It is sometimes amazing to observe the insurmountable difficulty a cultured professional person may experience when trying to understand simple concepts that were not previously registered in his intellectual equipment. Nevertheless, integration progresses constantly, although after the age of thirty, very few qualities are integrated.

The other shaping process, one which is closely related to anguish and the capacity for self-control, is that of learning. The learning process covers all the acquisitions and changes that take place during growth. A large part of it is accomplished through imitation, that is, by deliberate or unconscious copying of others' behavior, so that other people's modes of adjustment are incorporated into the personality.

The psychoanalytic concept of the personality consists of the following four parts:

1) The Unconscious
2) The Subconscious or "Id"
3) The Ego
4) The "Super-Ego"

If we imagine our mind to be a lake, the bottom is equivalent to the unconscious. The unconscious is really our psychological and physiological heritage. It is governed by the secretion of our endocrinal glands, our inheritance, the composition of our blood, our nation of origin, the social and religious environment, customs and tendencies, our culture and all the millions of preceding human experiences. Its' roots go as far back as man's first appearance on earth. The unconscious is the instinctive, inferior and primitive foundation in man.

As an intermediary between the unconscious and the ego, there is the subconscious or "id." It's roots are to be found in the unconscious, so that it is closely related to it. Together, both make up the deposit of the instincts, customs and memories. The "id" is neither moral nor immoral, as the ensemble of our tendencies, instincts and desires are grouped together in it. It has no knowledge of social, family or ethical conventionalism and tends to satisfy its own organic and psychic needs as quickly as possible. These needs are known by the name of "compulsions." Compulsions are tendencies that spring from the subconscious and which demand the fulfillment of a particular need.

The ego, in terms of psychology, is that part of the "id" that has been transformed by external circumstances. It aids the individual's adaptation and teaches him to recognize the demands of reality.

Above the sphere of the ego, resides the "super-ego" or censure, which in a way is the individual's moral conscience. It is shaped primarily in childhood, when the individual assimilates the cultural norms of conduct. For Freud, however, the "super-ego" is not superior to the ego from the moral point of view, because it is formed as an imposition of society. The "super-ego" is inhibited by education and social conventionalism and is the part of the ego that has been capitalized upon by educators. It works by setting in motion certain prohibitions, which unleash the mechanism of repression. Repression arises as a consequence of the struggle between the "id" and the "super-ego."

The subconscious or "id" is physiologically manifested through the thalamus, which is an area of neural activity located underneath the brain. The thalamus and neighboring regions are the center of the instincts, emotions, pain, customs and moods. The region of the thalamus is the great regulator of the brain and the whole sympathetic nervous system depends upon it. The individual's conscious part is represented in the upper cerebral cortex, the seat of the mind, of conscience, and will; the center which regulates, controls and harmonizes. The thalamus is the center of emotional and subconscious compulsions. When the cerebral cortex is not working properly, the impulses of the thalamus are left to their own devices, no longer submitted to the control of the cortex, and the individual finds himself submitted to compulsions, emotions, fits of rage, and aggression.

The repression mechanism is set in motion when an impulse that is in conflict with one's morals or education comes from the subconscious. Such an impulse, which slides electrically towards the cerebral cortex, encounters censure or the "super-ego" repressing it on the way. The individual may still be unaware of its existence because it does not reach the cerebral cortex. This compulsion drifts towards the sympathetic nervous system, which once perturbed, gives rise to anguish.

To sum up, each person has a particular psychic mechanism that he or she uses to face the environment.

The personality is the map of each person's mental mechanisms. This design is an ensemble of circuits that allows the intelligence of the individual to express itself.

CONSCIOUSNESS AND HYPSOCONSCIOUSNESS

HypsoConsciousness, (where "hypso" means elevated) is a term I have introduced to describe a scientific, rational, and physiological explanation for the diverse functional disturbances that occur in the human being which have a tremendous importance and a decisive influence on his life. These disturbances concern his inability to use his intellectual faculties effectively to solve his emotional conflicts, to live in the real world, to know the truth, to remove himself from the harmful effects of stress, to keep the collective peace, and in general, to solve all those things that demand the perfect functioning of his brain, together with a certain human quality.

Theoretically, the possession of intelligence should enable the human being to solve his problems successfully. What is it that happens inside him which transforms him into a fickle entity, subject to circumstances, to his emotions and impulses? Why is it that the formidable structure of man's brain does not enable him to deal with the environment in a really comprehensive way?

By using the psychological concepts from the previous chapters in addition to others introduced in this chapter, we will discover the mechanism that prevents man from fully utilizing his intelligence.

There is only one fundamental element that causes the notable and unsuspected decline of the human mind; A LOW LEVEL OF CONSCIOUSNESS. The basic nature of one's psychic life is consciousness, which encompasses every aspect of one's entire life.

Warren's Dictionary of Psychology gives the following definitions of Consciousness:
1) "Consciousness is the feature that distinguishes psychic life, diversely characterized as: a) perception in general; b) central effect of neural reception; c) the capacity to experience; d) subjective aspect of cerebral activity; e) relationship of the "I" with the environment."

2) "Total sum of an individual's experiences at a given moment."

3) "Capacity of the individual to know external objects and influence them."

4) "Attitude of the individual towards the moral or social implications of his own behavior which implies a value judgement."

In reference to these definitions it is obvious that the entire existence of consciousness is developed around the "I." The "I" is the essential point of reference for the individual. It is the exact point of union between the past and the future. The "I" should always be considered as indissolubly united with consciousness. In view of the intangible nature and difficulty in evaluating psychic phenomena however, I hope to show as much as possible that in most individuals, consciousness *"functions"* without the "I," or without a mature, stable "I."

Let's begin by dividing consciousness into two main states well known to everyone, sleep and wakefulness. For the moment, it will be better to leave aside the definition of these states in order to examine the total phenomenon of consciousness.

Compare consciousness to the scale on a thermometer. Imagine a scale of 20 degrees, in which 10 are above zero and 10, below. The degrees above zero represent the state of wakefulness and those below, the state of sleep. It is well known that there are several degrees of depth in sleep which have not been defined and classified into utilizable concepts. It is never considered that just as there are diverse degrees of depth in sleep, there are also several degrees of depth in wakefulness, thus enabling a person to be more or less awake in his normal activity.

Returning to the analogy of the thermometer, the degrees of heat (above zero) would be assigned to awakeness, and the degrees of cold (below zero) to sleep. In the case of temperature, two different phenomena do not exist, that is, one called heat and the other cold, but only one called temperature. Zero is only an arbitrary division in order to judge a thermic manifestation according to scale.

At the practical level, this means that there is still coldness at 10° above zero and heat at 50° below zero. When we say 20° above zero, we mean that there is *less cold* than at 0° and by 50° below zero, we mean that there is *less heat* than at 0°.

Likewise, we should consider sleep and wakefulness as a similarly unique phenomenon, that is, as different degrees of consciousness. Thus, on the scale of consciousness, sleep and wakefulness mingle; the arbitrary zero only represents the moment at which we fall asleep, and, to express it poorly, "lose consciousness."

There is an apparent state of wakefulness of a physiological nature that is marked by the absence of the phenomena present during sleep, and another, more profound state of wakefulness which is difficult to recognize and which concerns cerebral and mental activity. Using our scale of consciousness, we shall call this state "authentic wakefulness" or "awakeness" in order to differentiate it from physiological wakefulness, which we shall call "apparent wakefulness."

Due to the complexity and novelty of this phenomenon, it is necessary to specify how certain terms will be used in order to avoid confusion. Whenever we talk about "being awake," we shall be referring to "a state of awareness and alert watchfulness."

Into this psychic complex we need to introduce the concepts of "conscious" and "subconscious" in order to name a third element called the *"supraconscious."* In the way in which the first two terms are considered in traditional psychology, they cannot be applied to the total schema of the scale of consciousness, until the third element which we shall call "supraconscious" is added. The supraconscious, the conscious and the subconscious cannot be given a fixed position on the scale because its range varies according to the individual's mental activity. Only an attempt to specify those elements of consciousness that make up each of these parts can be made, and to this end an extensive analysis of the phenomenon of the "I" is necessary.

What is the "I?" The "I" is usually defined as "one's own identity," that is, as something that persists throughout a lifetime without any essential change. We shall define the concept of "I" as it relates to man's more concrete and definitive faculties, thus fully corresponding to the theory of levels of consciousness expounded in HypsoConsciousness.

The "I" is the sum of the individual's conscious reflective learning.

Apparently, the "I" is merely a different name for the personality. The very idea of the personality as something unique and different in each person leads one to identify it with the "I". Actually, we shall prove through HypsoConscious analysis that *the "I" is exactly the opposite of the personality.*

Let us divide the individual into two basic mechanisms: the "I" and the "we." The "we" in this case has a different meaning to that given by Fritz Kunkel. We will consider the "we" as synonymous with the personality, that is, as an indication of the overwhelming influence that the social group exerts on the individual, whom it shapes, models and transforms. The "we" is that which is not the individual's "own." It is the direct or indirect influence of other minds that penetrate the individual's own mind without him being able to oppose or withdraw from such pressures.

On the other hand, the "I" is all that which is the individual's own. It is that part of the cultural and environmental influence that he deliberately chose, and which he transformed, enlarged and incorporated according to his own criterion. The true "I" is always shaped on the strength of reflection and intelligent analysis of the facts.

The "I" exists in all individuals but remains beyond the functional mechanism of the intellect. Moreover, it is not a mature, developed, adult "I," but a minimized, frail and asthenic one. Every individual has acquired some fragments of conscious learning, which is what has shaped his or her "I."

We have defined the "I" as "the sum of the individual's conscious reflective learning." Remember that we are not referring to the "I" in its current psychological sense. In this case, "I" is capitalized and is in quotation marks. It is the true "I" that should be inherent to our human condition, not the pseudo-I, without quotation marks, which pertains only to barely conscious beings who do not know how to use their creative intelligence.

Most people whose "I's" are not made up of the sum of their conscious reflective learning do not possess an "I" in the strict sense of the word, but merely a "we." The "I" exists in other individuals, but in a minimal state, since its ensemble of conscious experiences is very limited in scope.

What is it that enables some people to have an authentic "I" and others not? The answer is in *learning*, because learning is the architect that builds the human mental edifice. Through the following explanation, it is apparent that it does not matter so much *what* a person learns, but *how* he or she learns it.

We can differentiate five different types of learning: *Unconscious learning; Unconscious reflective learning; Conscious learning; Conscious reflective learning; Superconscious reflective learning.*

Unconscious learning is that which is attained mainly through conditioning, imitation and influence. Together with unconscious reflective learning, it shapes the subconscious.

Unconscious reflective learning occurs when the individual reflects in detail on concepts or experiences, but while his level of alertness is low. However, can a person who is using his intelligence be unconscious? By examining the scale of consciousness, it can be seen that it only indicates the degrees of wakefulness, degrees through which the individual fluctuates. Throughout the process, the individual does not lose his reasoning faculties although they are distorted by the influence of the oneiric state. Does the individual not think and reflect while he sleeps? These matters will be discussed in greater depth still further on.

Conscious learning happens when an individual possesses a high level of wakefulness, but to a certain extent, lacks reflective power or does not use it properly.

Conscious reflective learning occurs when a person with a higher than usual level of consciousness or awareness, uses in addition to that, his reflective power.

Finally, *superconscious reflective learning* is achieved when the individual accomplishes, through a method, a high level of consciousness, and furthermore utilizes his reflective power correctly.

Conscious learning and conscious reflective learning together make up the individual's consciousness, while superconscious reflective learning makes up the supraconscious. Very few people possess the supraconscious which represents an individual's maximum fulfillment.

One very important fact springs to mind when considering the different states of consciousness: both the oneiric state as well as the state of wakefulness are mingled in the brain at the same time and exert an influence on its mechanism. The individual is never entirely asleep or entirely awake. During the day, there is always a certain dose of the oneiric state present in the state of wakefulness. At night, when a person dreams, he always possesses a certain state of consciousness.

In order to appreciate the degree of functional perturbation brought on in the brain by the oneiric state, one should briefly consider mental activity during sleep. The world of dreams has no logic, proportion or rational intelligence. The events that take place during sleep are quite at odds with the individual's real life. There is no subjection to physical or moral laws. It is the world of the absurd and the illogical in which fantasy reigns. The higher faculties of the mind momentarily undergo obliteration and only the instinctive and emotional forces come into play. The individual reasons, but this process is completely distorted under the oneiric influence. "Distortion" is what commonly happens in the human mind. A person may reflect laboriously but his reasoning suffers a distortion due to the capricious and inconstant influence of the oneiric atmosphere which is always present. The average person is incapable of living fully within reality. This phenomenon is what we call "a low level of consciousness." Anybody with a low level of consciousness remains in a profound oneiric state. Those individuals with a higher level of consciousness have within their psyches, a weaker oneiric state. In order to emphasize the tremendous importance this has, we shall maintain the following: "The degree of functional perfection of the human mind is in direct proportion to a higher level of consciousness and inversely proportional to a low level of consciousness."

The higher the level of consciousness, the more capable the person will be of attaining the full functioning of his intellectual abilities, of living in the real world, of overcoming his inner conflicts, and of knowing the truth.

This phenomenon is ignored in traditional psychology as is everything concerning the authentic "I," but it is doubtless the most important key to explaining the disconcerting and variable reactions of human behavior.

The relationship between consciousness and

intelligence is germane to this discussion. Note, when we speak of the word "consciousness," we are referring to a high level of consciousness. Consciousness and intelligence are not the same. It is moreover curious to observe how often an extremely cultured and learned man can have a lower level of awakeness than an uneducated laborer. The learned man to a great extent lacks a genuine "I," because he possesses voluminous cultural equipment, and the influence of the social group is pervasive and strong in him, so that he has a lot that is not "his own" and his "we" predominates in his mind. What the simple man of limited experience and culture possesses is almost exclusively his own. In other words, he possesses more "I" than "we."

These simple concepts were discovered by ancient philosophers in their yearning for truth. They understood that if knowledge is to be valid, it must be adjusted to truth and that wisdom is the perfect form of knowledge. *And when does an individual become wise?* When he is able to see things as they really are beyond mere appearances, thus transcending the oneiric restriction.

This theory of the level of consciousness

unfortunately suggests that we human beings were victims of a gigantic fraud because a portion of our minds (influenced by the oneiric state) interferes with the proper functioning of our brain. We live in just such a world where intelligent people are created, however, unfortunately with very low levels of consciousness. The subtlety of oneiric interference is such that by reflecting upon this matter, it is easily understood just how difficult it is for someone to study an intangible mechanism of a mental nature, especially when one considers that his own thoughts are not free from this interference. In order for an individual to be able to study and fully understand this phenomenon, he must begin by freeing his intelligence of the disturbing influence of the fanciful world of dreams.

CAUSES AND CONSEQUENCES OF A LOW LEVEL OF CONSCIOUSNESS

The basic cause of a low level of consciousness is without a doubt the under-development of the authentic "I", to which an endless number of diverse and variable factors contribute. We shall analyze these factors below by returning to our definition of the "I":

The "I" is the sum of one's conscious reflective learning and the "I" as counterposed to the "we," is all that is the individual's own. To clarify this further, we shall define the person with a fully grown and mature "I" as an *INDIVIDUAL,* and the one who only has a "we" as an *ANTI-INDIVIDUAL,* as seen in the following relationships:

Conscious Reflective Learning = "I" = Individual = A High Level of Consciousness.

Unconscious Learning = "WE" = Anti-individual = A Low Level of Consciousness.

The anti-individual is the natural product of man's passive submission to group behavioral patterns. A hedonistic attitude leads a person to systematically avoid the meditation of facts or ideas that are not in accordance with his usual approach. It is easier to let oneself be led by the crowd and adopt its habits, tastes and customs than it is to create one's own scale of values. This attitude reaches its extreme when a person lives in terms of the group's dictates, thus being incapable of psychic autonomy. He becomes just one more cog in a piece of gigantic machinery. The anti-individual is lazy in thought; he is not attracted to the reflective analysis of things; his thought is merely random. He is incapable of shaping a personal concept for himself of life, of human relationships or of the existence of God. He prefers to silently swallow the dogma put out by some religious and philosophical or political movements. He blindly accepts what science asserts or denies. If, for example, science states that telepathy is a fraud, then he does not bother to think further about it. He acknowledges the authority of the university without a shadow of a doubt. He is gullible enough to consider a university degree as an endowment of undeniable wisdom. He lives in constant fear of "what people will say" and molds his behavior according to the opinions of others. He is incapable of separating his knowledge from his beliefs and heatedly maintains a point of view merely because he is sure that "that's the way it is."

The anti-individual is at the same time both the cause and effect of a low level of consciousness. One cannot distinguish pure causes or effects in the mechanism of consciousness, since they mutually affect each other. Thus, for example, the two following assumptions are equally valid: "the anti-individual is a product of a low level of consciousness," and "a low level of consciousness is a consequence of being an anti-individual." The question is, which condition comes first? Is the low-level of consciousness a consequence of being an anti-individual or is the anti-individual the result of having a low level of consciousness?

Actually, a low level of consciousness precedes being an anti-individual. Conscious reflective learning is a means of shaping the mature "I". Yet how can a person learn consciously and reflectively if he does not possess a mature "I"? The concurrence of positive environmental factors during childhood, together with certain personal characteristics, yield an awakening of consciousness. Unfortunately, these elements are anti-social and anti-cultural in nature in that they break the bounds of established patterns. For example, a reserved child who has little contact with his schoolmates tends to be more reflective and observant and will meditate more profoundly on everything that penetrates his point of consciousness. This early intense use of the higher intellectual faculties shapes an "I" that develops rapidly to the degree in which the child persists in his analysis of his surrounding environment. The most important elements for the shaping of a high level of consciousness in a child are exposure to frequent changes and enriching experiences under the guidance of parents adept at stimulating the child's initiative and intellectual curiosity, together with the child's own characteristics.

The application of special techniques in school would of course allow for the methodical teaching of a system for achieving a higher level of consciousness in children. But this would imply an understanding of the phenomenon of awareness on the part of the relevant authorities, who would first have had to accomplish it themselves.

The educational system's aim is to administer knowledge to the child, but not for a child to attain true comprehension of that knowledge. The child is obliged to study complicated elements without having first been taught *to think*.

It is necessary to clarify a few terms in order to be able to explain the mechanism of how knowledge is acquired. Certain words will be given a more complete and precise meaning in order to differentiate them from their common use which cannot be applied to the higher mental mechanisms.

> *"To know"* is not the same as ***"to comprehend."***
> *"To think"* is not the same as ***"to meditate."***

A person may know without comprehending, but he cannot comprehend without knowing. Comprehension is ultimately the final elaboration of a specific field of knowledge that enables one to come to solid and profound conclusions that are perfectly integrated in one's mind. Comprehension is the perfect form of knowledge. "Knowing" is merely the general impression of data or information that is either deeply or superficially filed in the memory. The man who "knows" can only express prefabricated concepts.

The man who comprehends can pass judgements. The anti-individual "knows"; the individual "comprehends."

It is well known that any process of profound understanding affects the integration of certain elements that are never forgotten. Correct comprehension of the theory of relativity, for example, shapes a clear image in the brain that is left there forever at the individual's disposal. "Knowing" is limited, because it does not encompass the whole picture. Comprehending enables one to set up comparisons and relationships that help to broaden, perfect, and delve deeper into concepts.

To think is not the same as to meditate. In this book, "meditation" is seen as a process of profound comprehension conducted in a state of awareness that is more heightened than usual. All human beings think; only a few meditate. Thought, in its normal manifestations, is a disordered, diffuse and random activity in which the subject is swept along and dominated by his imagination. It could be said that one does not "think" but is "obliged to think." The thinker is dominated by prejudices and beliefs, and by emotional, instinctive and passional states.

"To meditate," on the other hand, implies a

higher cerebral activity where the individual voluntarily, deliberately and consciously exercises his reasoning faculties. Mental clarity, a feature possessed by so few individuals, is crucial to the act of "meditation." One is unable to "think" clearly. The human being's usual mental state is more or less confused, vague and diffuse, even when applied to the intellectual solution of certain unknown factors.

To summarize, "thinking" is synonymous with "knowing" and "meditating" is synonymous with "comprehending."

Apparently, logic supplies us with the necessary elements to handle thought efficiently. Unfortunately, logic does not permit us to correct the errors caused by distorted concepts arrived at through insufficient or defective observation. The thoughts of our practical life are based on vague and undefined concepts. In reality, only in exceptional moments does man think with total mental clarity. The lack of mastery of the intellectual faculties is one of the chief causes of a low level of consciousness.

Another main cause of a low level of consciousness is the phenomenon called *"Identification."* Identification occurs when consciousness is absorbed into an idea, when it is drawn into an external or internal phenomenon, or when it is attracted by visual or auditory images or movements of a specific nature.

Imagine consciousness as a rubber ball that is attached to a person's forehead. In the circumstance of identification, consciousness, referring to a more or less heightened level of consciousness and here represented by the rubber ball, detaches itself to the degree that it is either attracted to or resists an external object. Suppose that this individual is sitting comfortably in an armchair, doing nothing in particular. Suddenly the glass of a window-pane is violently shattered by the impact of a stone. Right away, the rubber ball (his consciousness) is projected onto what happened, returning to him together with a sensory message that is not adequately interpreted or assimilated because the individual is "unconscious," that is, his judgment is momentarily obliterated. He therefore reacts violently, because he is unable to return to consciousness before he receives the sensory impact. Hence a typical case of "identification" or projection of the "I" is produced. This individual became a part of the phenomenon itself, thus feeling it with a special intensity. In other words, he "integrated himself" with the phenomenon of the shattering of the glass. Identification converts a man from a spectator into an actor, and he thus easily loses his balance.

Every day, people must face up to problems and events that don't directly concern them but which affect them emotionally to a great extent. The degree of identification with a particular problem will be proportional to the degree that one is disturbed by it.

For example, what happens if we see a person who has fainted lying unconscious in the street. What we see disturbs us to a certain degree. Suppose now that the unconscious person is a member of our family. In this case, we probably would feel profoundly disturbed because our resultant identification would be much greater due to the emotional ties.

The more "un-identified" we are with regard to a particular situation, the more we are able to reason clearly. It is relatively easy, for example, to advise a friend regarding the solution to a problem that he is unable to see clearly because of his total identification with it, while the reasons might be quite obvious to us. If on the other hand, this problem were our own, we probably would be incapable of solving it correctly. By comprehending the phenomenon of "identification," the key to attaining a state of serenity can be discovered and the following chapters will reveal techniques to that end.

There is a vicious cycle in the shaping and subsistence of a low level of consciousness, because it generates certain psychic states which in turn keep the individual in a state of sleep. Inner conflicts provoke and maintain a low state of awakeness by keeping one removed from reality. Complexes, frustrations, repression and neuroses are all mortal enemies of consciousness. In the same way, one's habits are a veritable barrier to attaining a high state of awakeness, because habits diminish the conscious attention necessary for carrying out one's tasks.

Any incapacity to awaken oneself is fundamentally a disturbance of the cerebral and mental functions. No one is really "normal" in the ideal sense; instead, all human beings are more or less influenced by compulsive impulses. All nervous disturbances are mental perturbations, and any mental perturbation upsets the normal functioning of the brain.

Normally, the reasoning faculty should suffice for the individual to control his negative emotional states and states of exaggerated tension. However, we often observe that highly intelligent people have no more control over themselves than others with a low IQ's.

The state of sleeping while appearing to be awake in many cases represents a prolongation of the fetal stage in which the future human being was asleep in the womb, protected and comfortable. The trauma of birth caused by the abrupt separation from the mother is often prolonged into adulthood and may stratify extensive areas of the personality at the childhood level. The individual never matures and is perpetually in search of something that will substitute the maternal image.

Often people with personalities lacking in nuances and experiences are more balanced and stable.

A man with a low state of consciousness of necessity suffers from exaggerated nervous tension, lack of self-control, fatigue, lack of concentration, a low level of productivity, etc.

THE CONSCIOUS
AND THE SUBCONSCIOUS

The mind is made up of a conscious part and a subconscious part. The classical representation of this division is the image of an iceberg, the great mass of which is submerged below the ocean's surface, while only a tiny portion rises above it. The subconscious part, to which we have no conscious and voluntary access, is like another person, an unknown, enigmatic, complex and irrational entity within the same individual. For the purpose of simplicity, no distinction will be made between the subconscious and the unconscious, since they are separated only by degrees of awakeness.

Conscious and unconscious thoughts display characteristic differences that make them easily distinguishable. Some of these differences are listed as follows:

Conscious thought:

- Follows the rules of logic.
- The sense of discrimination is clearly delineated.
- Is subject to social norms, regardless of what this subjection may cost the individual.
- Is governed by a sense of duty.
- Is based on reasoning and self-expression.

Unconscious thought:

- Possesses a logic that follows neither syllogistic norms nor the relationship of cause and effect.
- The critical function of differentiation is not clearly established.
- Respects only the individual's psycho-physical well-being, regardless of the consequences that this behavior might have on others.
- Is governed by the pleasure principle.
- Is built on the emotions and is developed through the repression of the emotions.

Even though the conscious and the subconscious represent two personalities within the human being, there is not a sharp and clearly delineated separation between the two. Both act together in the brain. The product of one's intellectual activity springs from the mixture of conscious and subconscious elements. By making a decision, for example, one can never really know the extent to which impulses or unconscious experiences have influenced the intellectual process. This intrusion of thoughts does not conform to the norms of logic and reasoning and may seriously harm the closeness of the intellect to truth, because the individual may be accepting as real elements which do not in any way fit in with reality.

Ask yourself if you are able to realize when your thoughts are conscious or unconscious. Even a superficial examination of this problem reveals the insurmountable difficulties that it presents. Are you able to examine yourself with your own instrument of knowledge in order to determine the degree of perfection or inaccuracy of your ability for analysis? Evaluating others presents the same problems because the analyst must begin by determining his own level of consciousness.

Should we consider subconscious intrusion as a functional disorder or view it simply as a natural, normal and necessary phenomenon? To reply to this question, we must return to our classification of humanity as "individuals" and "anti-individuals" and the possibility of attaining a "supraconscious" part.

The human being's relative free will, enables him to choose within certain limits what he wishes to attain in life. One cannot judge, criticize, or reproach those who vegetate in ignorance, who do not aspire to self-knowledge. Not everyone can be the same. There have to be anti-individuals, individuals, geniuses, boors, idlers, etc. For those who do not aspire to the knowledge of truth, a low level of consciousness must be considered as normal and necessary. On the contrary, those who feel that they have the ineluctable duty to surpass themselves with the aim of attaining complete fulfillment and maturity as individuals should consider subconscious perturbation as a phenomenon that they must of necessity overcome in order to progress.

Just as there are "anti-individuals," there are also "anti-men" who are not very far removed from the animal kingdom as far as consciousness is concerned. According to the theory of the level of consciousness, consciousness must be considered as that which distinguishes man from animal. The human quality in an individual has nothing to do with his intelligence. One may observe individuals of brilliant intelligence who are totally dominated by animal tendencies. _Dr. Jekyll and Mr. Hyde_ by Robert Louis Stevenson is a symbolic representation of the animal factor hidden in the unconscious.

It must be made clear, however, that the subconscious, just like a child, is neither good nor bad; it simply lacks judgment. The subconscious is credulous and malleable and is easily affected by external influences. In some way, the subconscious represents a prolongation of childhood. Where is the child we all once were? We generally consider childhood as a thing of the past that died to make way for the adult. The child is still alive, however, but is latent, and merely numbed by education. In moments of tension, the child emerges and takes over the direction of the brain, driving an individual to carry out irrational acts that are the product of childish reactions of fear, anger or love. It is this child that must be educated and disciplined if we are to become true adults with effective emotional and intellectual maturity.

We do not realize to what extent we are still children, to what extent we play with the things of life, in what ways we avoid reality, seeking shelter in the lap of a symbolical mother, numbing ourselves with childish dreams. A person can seldom face up to life as it is and look reality in the face without entering into an imaginary world created to suit his own tastes. This happens in order to appease the anxiety of the child who faces a wide world in which he feels alone, destitute and defenseless. Only the true adult can live in reality and know the world for what it is, without decorating it in order to better withstand it.

The child within plays nasty tricks on the individual that usually interfere with his conscious projects. One's health or illness depend to a great extent on this child, as do one's prosperity or downfall, success or failure.

In a fit of terror this child, without a sense of judgment, can blind, confound, or paralyze us. Under better circumstances, he celebrates our success. It is capable of systematically preventing us from earning money or it can help us to earn it. If it is actively interested in our projects, we will certainly succeed. If it is indifferent, we will advance at a snail's pace or not at all. Paradoxically, this being that is without judgment or reason, is our master in many ways and controls an extensive area of the brain. It knows more than our conscious "I." It is the archive in which all events that have happened to us, all fleeting comparisons and all subliminal observations are kept. We can do nothing without the permission and help of the subconscious. If it does not approve of any enterprise, then we shall certainly fail. If it gives us its support, then we are sure to succeed. There are countless testimonies from people who suffered serious physical disorders brought on by their subconscious in a childish attempt to avoid certain unpleasant facts.

Many psychosomatic illnesses are brought on by the evasion of elements that deeply disturb the individual and which find a plausible justification in an illness in order to avoid facing reality.

The power of the subconscious is so great over our lives that we believe we have been helped by God when really we have used our faith in a divine being as a means for achieving certain things. Of course, if we profoundly and truly believe in something, we are gaining the cooperation of our subconscious. Dr. John

Pfeiffer observed this phenomenon in his book _The Human Brain_: "A volunteer is hypnotized and told that his hand will be touched with a red-hot iron; he is prepared for the worst and the worst comes. It does not matter if the hypnotist uses a pencil or his own finger, or a piece of ice instead of a red-hot iron, because the effect is the same. The volunteer shouts with pain and pulls his hand away. The expectation of the burn is such that it produces exactly the same changes as a real burn would produce in the organism. A colorless fluid flows from the blood vessels to the hand and emerges through the 'injured' zone. The liquid causes real blisters that are just as lasting and painful as those produced by an actual hot iron." This phenomenon was produced exclusively by the action of the subconscious on the body. The state of hypnosis, as will be explained later, is merely when a person is at a very low level of consciousness.

However, there exists yet an even more interesting phenomenon. If a post-hypnotic suggestion was given to a hypnotized subject that by touching him with a finger he was really being burned by a red-hot iron, the results would certainly be the same as if it really were a red-hot iron, and, the subject, even though awake and conscious, would have fallen victim to an irresistible corroboration with the mechanisms of his subconscious. By properly understanding that this influence can only be exerted on the strength of belief, one can realize with a certain trepidation the tremendous power that one's own deeply rooted beliefs can hold over oneself.

Consider what happens when the level of consciousness is heightened. Raising it always implies a reduction in the field of mental activity that is controlled by the subconscious, and an enlargement of the field of mental activity controlled by the conscious part. In other words, to raise the level of consciousness is to endow the subconscious with consciousness. It means keeping "the child" under control in a way. The child thus becomes subject to our control as long as we manage to maintain a high level of consciousness. This is, in part, the aim of HypsoConsciousness.

HYPNOSIS

Hypnosis is usually thought of as something remote that does not directly affect one's daily life. At the mere mention of the word, one immediately thinks of theatrical shows in which the "magician" obliges selected subjects to carry out a series of laughable, outlandish acts. The human being does not for one moment accept that he is in some way directly and personally involved in the diversity of hypnotic phenomena. Hypnosis actually forms an inseparable part of our psychic life from the moment of birth.

Scant knowledge of the truly scientific aspect of hypnosis, leads people to consider it as merely a process that takes place between the hypnotist and the hypnotized subject, in which the latter briefly loses his will and judgment. Nevertheless, it is no more than the conscious and deliberate provocation of the state of hypnosis. In its most frequent manifestation, hypnosis is a process that is manifested spontaneously under the pressure of certain natural hypnotic elements, or it can also be exerted unconsciously by some people.

Hypnosis is defined as an emotional reaction that brings about certain psycho-physiological changes.

There are two basic emotional states, that Dr. Walter Hess (Nobel Prize for Medicine 1949 for investigations on the brain) calls "ergotropic" and "trophotropic." The "ergotropic" state corresponds to a perturbed emotional reaction that is characterized by the stimulation of the sympathetic nervous system. The "trophotropic" state corresponds to a stabilizing emotion in which the parasympathetic nervous system predominates.

Any hypnotic process of necessity has to be verified as either a perturbing or a stabilizing emotional reaction. The earliest and simplest hypnotic state is that experienced by the infant when it is caressed and nursed by its mother, thus producing a state of relaxation, in addition to regulating its organic processes. The correct balance between relaxing and alarming stimuli is the key for the normal development of the personality. Many different experiences and observations have established that when the maternal hypnotic stimulus is lacking, the child's normal development is impeded, so that he is left with serious physical and mental deficiencies, and in some cases, even death.

Hypnosis always represents an intensified emotional state, whether it be stabilizing or perturbing. The techniques of hypnotic induction shed much light on the spontaneous and unconscious modalities of the hypnotic process. All of them without exception resort to concentrating the subject's attention on something. In antiquity, for example, hypnotists hypnotized their subjects perhaps by producing a violent stimulus, such as striking a gong combined with the imperative order to sleep. Other procedures fixed the individual's attention by auditory or visual stimuli. In order to induce a positive or stabilizing state in the subject, the hypnotist uses a variety of suggestions to provoke a state of physical and emotional relaxation.

Emotions can have varying degrees of intensity. These degrees of intensity correspond to the depth of hypnosis. At each degree, several changes in behavior are produced that affect the subject's intellectual faculties and normal reactions. Some of these changes, in order of hypnotic depth are as follows: alterations in the physical functions, exaltation of the imagination, hallucinations, analgesia, spontaneous catalepsy, reduction and annulment of contact with the outer world and finally, "suspended animation," or a state of lethargy with metabolic, respiratory and circulatory depression. Hypnosis is really a form of emotional shock.

In his _Introduction to Psychology_, Piriz states that the crucial psychological factor in the human mass lies in his emotions, "which when exalted, is inversely proportioned to intellectual and volitive life, lessening the individual's capacity for criticism and the functions of higher conscience. The individual then suffers a state of hyper-suggestibility and a greater susceptibility to imitation." Freud defined deliberate hypnosis as "a collective formation of only two people."

Returning to the theory of the level of consciousness, hypnosis shall be defined as a profound drop in the level of consciousness provoked by the immediate or gradual retention of the subject's attention. Thus the hypnotized subject's behavior closely resembles the characteristics of unconscious thought.

To hypnotize a person involves bringing the child within him to the surface, so that it can be easily influenced, because it lacks intellectual maturity. How do we persuade a child to do something? Naturally, we impose our will involving fear in an authoritarian way (ergotropic reaction), or else we calm him by offering some reward (trophotropic reaction).

Life generates a succession of perturbing and stabilizing emotional states revealing that the hypnotic state is inseparable from man's daily activity. Thus, subconscious forms of thought emerge with emotional states dominating over the higher functions of the intellect.

The modern world makes it particularly difficult for the human being to withdraw from the hypnotic state and for the "anti-individual" to transform himself into an individual. I refer to the irresistible cultural and emotional influence of the community and to certain technological advances. The mass absorbs the individual and passes on to him its emotional irradiation, hypnotizing him and submitting him to its constant emotional influence. Anatol Milechnin states that the "psycho-physiological behavior of individuals that make up the mass, is essentially the same as that which takes place in a deliberately induced hypnotic state of a certain profundity."

Gustav Le Bon, in his renowned work, _The Psychology Of The Masses_, speaks of the law of mental unity of the masses. We live in the era of the masses. Everything is organized according to political, economic, philosophical or religious groupings of individuals who are impotent to withdraw from the group influence. In it, he expounds interesting principles that are closely linked to this subject:

"... there is a psychological law of the mental unity of the masses ... The most astonishing fact displayed by a psychological mass is the following: that whoever are the individuals that make it up, and however alike or unlike their ways of life, their occupations, their character or intelligence might be, on account of the mere fact of becoming a mass, they possess a kind of collective soul that makes them think, feel and act in a completely different way to that in which they would think, feel or act each in isolation. . . The dissipation of the conscious personality, predomination of the unconscious personality, orientation via influence, contagion of feelings and ideas in the same sense, the tendency to immediately transform suggested ideas into acts, are then the main characteristics of the individual in a mass. The individual is not himself, but an automaton who is not governed by will."

The behavior of the mass, according to Le Bon's description, is provoked by a low level of consciousness, a hypnotic state that annuls the faculties of judgement, criticism and discrimination. Thus, individual intelligence is not enough to enable a person to free himself from the hypnotic influence of the community, unless it is accompanied by a high level of consciousness, whether this be deliberate or spontaneous. Political and religious collectives are especially effective in preventing their followers' intellectual autonomy. Moreover, these followers, as everybody knows, are under the broader, more powerful influence of the whole of humanity, especially as far as its form of culture and organization are concerned.

Thus, the hypnotic state is inherent to the human being's "normal" existence. Those however, who for various reasons, succeed in becoming real "individuals," attain thereby the true inheritance of human beings who possess consciousness.

Humanity today in no way represents the peak of the species' evolution, which hasn't even met the half-way mark towards its evolutionary goal. The human being reveals himself as an incomplete structure, one that is only half-realized. We should not forget that the conscious behavior of the human species on earth goes no further back than ten or twenty thousand years, as opposed to a hundred or a hundred and fifty thousand years of unconscious behavior; or perhaps even millions of years if we consider the course of evolution of the species from the beginning of the simplest form of life.

Hypnosis always represents a state of fascination exerted over the subject's mind, a result of his attention being held by lasting or changing stimuli. The elements of our civilized life are endowed with a powerful hypnotic influence. The term "fascination" says a lot in itself. How many "fascinating" things are there in the world today?

Everything goes against the attainment of a high level of consciousness. The press, cinema, television, radio, publicity, shop-windows, political and religious indoctrination, all cover up a well organized conspiracy aimed at maintaining hypnotic sleep. The use of bright colors, shiny metals, neon advertisements, whimsical architectural forms, and the interminable succession of visual images keep the individual "mentally trapped." However, the real mechanisms of hypnosis are produced within the individual's psychic sphere and in particular in the imaginative field. Thus, the intellectual or scientist who delights in high-brow reflections is just as much, or perhaps even more so, hypnotized than a television fanatic. The kaleidoscopic imaginative flow keeps him "fascinated" and enchanted by the plastic world that lends itself to infinitely varied images. The stimuli that set it in motion can be external or internal. To flee from civilization in order to evade hypnosis, is no remedy at all, for our own thoughts are equally efficient at hypnotizing us.

We live in a world of hypnotized beings in which the leaders are "hypnotized hypnotists" who have developed highly charged emotional states and who are often fanatics, hallucinators or single-minded people themselves.

On the other hand, a lack of stimuli disturbs the functioning of the cerebral cortex, making people irritable, easily impressionable and subject to visual and audio hallucinations. Only by keeping a high level of consciousness can the individual attain adequate emotional homeostasis, correct adaptation to the environment and a full yield of his intellectual faculties.

To sum up, the individual is constantly submitted to hypnosis by external influences or else to "self-hypnosis" through fixed ideas that exert control over his mind. The state of hypnosis always represents a low level of consciousness and implies predomination of the subconscious over the conscious, that is, a predomination of the child over the adult.

One of the main obstacles to attaining a high level of consciousness is the emotional symbiosis produced between mother and child. This hypnotic relationship creates firm suggestive links that generally withstand the passage of time. The once child is left in a state of dependency upon the maternal image that is very closely linked to stabilizing emotional reactions. In childhood, the stabilizing maternal influence represents the means for avoiding inevitable disturbing emotional states encountered by the child in his gradual contact with his environment. The mother symbolizes a sort of fortress in which to shelter himself from negative emotional circumstances. When he reaches adulthood, the child has great difficulty in becoming independent from the symbiosis with his mother and generally seeks a symbolic substitution for her. The crowd represents the mother, for the individual feels protected by his anonymity within it, free of responsibility and safe from the obligation of assuming his own modes of behavior. He may thus reach old age and still be a child. It is possible that the "second childhood" observed in old people may be no more than a weakening of the "adult attitude" that life obliges them to adopt. When he reaches old age, the individual simply behaves like the child he has always been.

REAL EXISTENCE
AND FANCIFUL EXISTENCE

The oneiric world and the world of wakefulness are the two basic spheres of the activity of consciousness which fluctuates cyclically between these two extremes. There is no real marked division between either state, rather only differentiation by degrees in the level of consciousness. When one sleeps, one is less conscious than in the awake state; when awake, one is more conscious. This does not mean that the individual is totally awake in his awake state, since there are as many degrees of wakefulness as there are of sleep. Actually, people's habitual state of awakeness is mediocre and one can only consider oneself to be awake in relation to when one sleeps deeply with a loss of consciousness.

The state which is wrongly called "conscious" is

really a *hypoconscious* state, and the "I" with which people normally function is a *hypoconscious* "I" which should be strictly included in the subconscious.

Within the mind there exists two "I's": the "Superior I" and the "inferior I." The "Superior I" is conscious and the "inferior I" is *hypoconscious.* The "inferior I" is sufficient for acting in normal life, so much so that years may go by without one ever making contact with the "Superior I."

The true "I," as defined in this work, is a capitalized "I"; it is the "Superior I," the product of the individual's reflective conscious learning. As mentioned before, the "I" and the "we" are considered as opposite factors; the "I" is "what is the individual's own," and the personality, that is the "we," is what is "not one's own" or as an imposing structure copied from the community mold.

Consider in detail the true meaning of individuality. When a person is not self-defined, but influenced by the dictates of the mass through its vast cultural and emotional influence, he stops existing as an individual and becomes integrated in the crowd whose irrational behavior has already been analyzed here. The instinctive, emotional and irrational mass which mentally functions in an unreal world, is the product of the collective unconscious and of the oneiric sphere which are inseparable from low levels of consciousness. Thus, when the anti-individual says "I," he really means "we." His "habitual I" is really an impostor, a "pseudo-I" which is merely an emotional-cultural projection of the community.

The anti-individual, dominated by the "inferior I" or "we," has no real existence of his own, but is merely a group reflection. TO TRULY BE, implies being fully conscious of existing as an individual. Hamlet's query, "To be or not to be," shows itself to be charged with unsuspected psychological and philosophical depth.

There are many elements which prevent a person from leading a real existence, but all of them act in the same way. They prevent the development and manifestation of the "Superior I." Unreal existence must always be considered in relation to the "I," in as far as the individual is able to say, "I am."

Perhaps the most important factor of a fanciful existence is "displacement" in time. Consciously, the individual adjusts his daily activity to time and has a sense of placement in space and time. This does not occur in the subconscious in which past, present and future co-exist. The time factor disappears completely during sleep and in thirty seconds a person can dream of events that cover an entire lifetime.

The influence of the "inferior I" or "subconscious I" is manifested in relation to the time phenomenon as an incapacity to live in the present moment. The subject's consciousness is projected to the past or the future, or else it is divided. An inability to live in the present moment means not being able to concentrate one's conscious faculties on the exact point of union between the past and the future, that is, the present moment.

If at a given moment a person's consciousness is not projected into the present, it is as if he does not exist, SINCE THE ONLY REALITY IS THE PRESENT MOMENT. The past and the future have no real existence NOW. The human being habitually lives projected towards the past and the future and therefore towards an unreal, fanciful existence.

Complexes are a clear manifestation of the

projection and fixation of consciousness on the past, and nervous tension, of the projection to the future. A shy person observes no difference between the humiliating experiences he is undergoing now and those he underwent in childhood. Actually, the emergence of his shyness now takes him back into the past which becomes united with the present.

Nervous tension is the anxious perception of the passing of time. The individual projects his "I" into the future trying to guess what will happen in anticipation of solving any problems that may arise. This becomes a bad habit and the individual constantly lives in expectation of what is coming to him and anguishes at the thought of the unknown, as illustrated in the following two examples.

John is having breakfast. It is exactly 8 o'clock in the morning. He is worried because he got up late and must get to work at a certain time. He has a difficult day ahead of him and he feels great emotional tension due to a vague, subconscious anticipation of everything that he has to do. He may possibly get up from the breakfast table at five past eight, kiss his wife and get into his car. All of this is already executed in his thoughts in an uninterrupted manner, intertwined with other actions foreseen in advance. In other words, what he is doing in the present moment is intertwined with what he must do in the future. While it is true that John has a car, and must go to work, nevertheless, at eight o'clock in the morning, the only reality is that he is having breakfast. At this time, what he supposedly should be doing later, is merely a future project. Whatever is not in direct contact with the present moment in which a person lives, is fanciful and unreal in relation to the "I." The car that John will get into at five past eight does not exist for him as long as it does not coincide with the present time. His "I" has been completely projected into the future, obliging him to exist fancifully or to not exist at all.

In the second example, Charles, who possesses an immature or undeveloped "I," is in his office writing a business letter, something he has done habitually for several years. While he writes, he has a vague awareness of other people around him; he feels very hot; he notices that his shirt-collar is too tight; he knows that he is sitting uncomfortably and is still influenced by an argument that he had with his boss that morning. Meanwhile, another part of his mind is working actively in an attempt to solve the economic problem he has to face the next day and he simultaneously feels that he is unhappy and should be working in another job. How long has all of this taken? Possibly less than a second, a time lapse in which Charles was mentally projected into the past, present and future. Moreover, his "I" followed this mental trip. It was really his "I" that was projected, resulting in a separation between the "I" and the physical execution of his present activity.

The human being is easily hypnotized by his own ideas and by external perceptions which lead him straight to the oneiric world, so that his "I" stops existing in objective reality.

Again, the incapacity to live in the present is caused by the inability to concentrate the "I" on the present moment. This establishes yet another difference between the "inferior I" and the "Superior I." The "Superior I" is perfectly integrated and has indivisible unity; the "inferior I" is divisible into countless little "I's" that are poorly integrated. The "inferior I" is the one that is projected into countless portions, each of which follows a different current of mental activity. The "Superior I" is the "I" of mental concentration, fully aware of the present moment, and the one that processes things in an orderly manner, one after another.

Apparently, projection to the future would seem to indicate that one should not plan things to come. A brief analysis, however, shows that any mental activity, whether it is directed to the past, present or future, becomes the activity of the present moment if the individual concentrates his "I" on this task to the exclusion of any other physical activity; that is, the individual is exclusively devoted to planning a future activity in the present moment.

In order to live in the present moment, it is absolutely necessary that the person concentrate all of his physical and mental activity on the present instant. To think of one thing while physically doing another is counterproductive, because it breaks psycho-physical unity, driving the functioning of mind and body into two different activities, so that a division is produced. There must be perfect unity between thought and action for the "Superior I" to properly manifest itself.

FATIGUE AND WORK

The separation of thought and action is disastrous, since it results in an over-squandering of nervous energy due to the simultaneous existence of opposing attitudes. There are often marked conflicts when it comes to making important decisions, because one wishes to attain one thing while at the same time wishing to avoid other things. This co-existence of one "acquisitive" attitude and another "evasive" one counterpoises two contrary volitive impulses which bring about an excessive waste of nervous energy. The following examples illustrate this more clearly.

A person is strolling absent-mindedly along the street, carrying a parcel in his hand. Suddenly, the parcel falls to the ground. He is at once faced with two opposing impulses: on the one hand, he is annoyed at having to bend down to pick it up and really does not wish to, but on the other hand, he knows that he should pick it up and he does so. In this apparently very simple act, he has spent an exorbitant amount of energy because he picked up the parcel against his wishes because he was obliged to.

This example illustrates the underlying principle of the law of fatigue and waste: "The greater psychic and physical unity there is in any task, the less waste of energy this will cause, and vice-versa." This explains why any task that is executed reluctantly tires one rapidly. The state of mental concentration applied to a specific activity, considerably slows down fatigue and increases personal efficiency.

Many people who have routine jobs that do not require a great effort, end their day's work in a considerable state of exhaustion, despite the shortness of their working day. On the other hand, those who do creative work can markedly lengthen their working day without feeling tired. Creative work demands a special concentration of the intellectual faculties. The pleasure principle increases efficiency and slows down fatigue in any activity. However, pleasure does not arise spontaneously because someone enjoys doing something, but often derives from their doing something well. When a person approaches a task impeccably, he enjoys doing it, particularly if this task is then admired and appreciated by other people. Thus, a person who plays golf very well enjoys mastering something beyond the reach of most people. This helps him to value himself and place himself on a high level within the group. Healthy self-esteem is one of the most powerful human needs and is indispensable to a normal existence in society.

An interesting experience would be to allow

yourself to feel pleasure while doing a task that you usually find annoying. To your surprise you may discover that what formerly tired you and got on your nerves, now helps you to relax and rest. By virtue of the union attained between mind and body, an individual's interest in the subject helps him to correctly and easily accomplish any task.

The human being uses up a greater amount of nervous energy than he needs to. Chronic fatigue, mental exhaustion, physical and nervous weakness, neurosis and many asthenic states basically represent a lack of energy because of excessive over-squandering. It is very common for people who lead a normal life without any particular physical or mental demands to feel constantly tired, which they generally attribute to physical ailments. The main problem of many individuals centers around a lack of imaginative discipline, which drives them to diffuse, disordered activity that disperses and uses up their energies. Of course, the low level of consciousness is always the first and foremost cause of most human problems.

RELAXATION

When one settles down to sleep, one instinctively practices relaxation. To fall asleep, what is necessary is a previous attitude of relaxation which will facilitate a tranquil and replenishing sleep.

Edmund Jacobson is credited with the creation of what is termed "scientific relaxation." His technique is based upon raising one's awareness of one's muscular contractions to thus voluntarily bring about relaxation. J.H. Schultz, the German neurologist, developed another method, generally considered to be more profound and complete, based on the deliberate induction of a state of self-hypnosis. These two authors, together with Kretschmer (creator of fractioned affective hypnosis) are the only ones who have explored the phenomenon of relaxation as a truly scientific technique, although generally only "Jacobson's method" or "Schultz's method" are mentioned.

The origin of relaxation is usually attributed to Hindu Yoga practices. While it is possible that Jacobson and Schultz may have been inspired by the abundant literature on Yoga, it would be a gross error to identify relaxation with Yoga, because relaxation is only a secondary consequence of a discipline that enables self-control and the elevation of the level of consciousness. Anybody who becomes an expert in self-control unknowingly practices relaxation. Animals can relax far more easily than human beings. For example, a cat remains relaxed, despite being alert.

All living beings with organic homeostatic powers possess the capacity for relaxation as proper and inherent to their existence, so that relaxation should really be identified with homeostatic power itself. We shall thus define voluntary relaxation as the deliberate and conscious management of a certain aspect of homeostatic power. Of course, the use of this technique presupposes a state of tension that must be surpassed in order to recover the lost balance.

Dr. Jacobson's relaxation technique is centered

on the musculature, correctly asserting that, "it is physically impossible to be nervous in a particular part of the body, if in that part one is totally relaxed." He states that if the skeletal muscles (the voluntary ones) are sufficiently relaxed, the internal muscles (those of the viscera) tend to be similarly relaxed. He also points out the difference between natural and scientific relaxation in which only the latter is able to make the residual tension in the muscles disappear, even when an individual is resting tranquilly. Naturally, as a specialist in physiology, Jacobson restricted his work to delegating relaxation itself to an imminently muscular process, excluding the psychological aspect. The neurologist, Schultz, on the other hand, centered his interest on the phenomenon of hypnosis, which inspired him to develop his "concentrative self-relaxation."

In this book, the phenomenon of relaxation is examined from a more integral point of view in order to elevate it's relevance as a technique for replenishing and maintaining organic, mental and emotional homeostasis, as well as being a shaping force for the new "supraconscious" psychological state that will enable the individual to attain perfect and complete fulfillment as a true human being.

Likewise, the true mechanism that enables one to attain "a personal attitude of relaxation" shall be explored in depth. Contrary to what is thought, relaxation is an active process, not a passive one. When one speaks of relaxation, one immediately thinks of something that leads a person to rest and then to sleep. The mental image we have of a relaxed person is one of total laxness and passivity. Even though certain pseudo-systems of relaxation aim at leading people to a state of total passivity, true and "noble" relaxation must be first and foremost an active process.

Eduardo Krapf, in his book, _Anguish, Tension and Relaxation_, says the following: "Relaxation that plays such a central part in sleep, has the nature of an active process." He later adds: "in other words, relaxation, far from being a phenomenon of laxness (on the periphery), is really an active process that emanates from the same person (which is the same as saying "the center"), that is, it is as different from the paralytic "hypotony" of the muscles that is usually observed in exhausted individuals, as sleep is from drowsiness or toxic coma."

HypsoConsciousness attempts, above all, to lead the person to a state of alertness rather than to one of sleep. From what is now known about the levels of consciousness, we can understand the way in which HypsoConsciousness operates. HypsoConsciousness (from the Greek, HYPSOS) is the term adopted to denote the essence of this method, that is, the elevation of consciousness, or rather the elevation of the LEVEL OF CONSCIOUSNESS. First of all, it is important to state again what this means, since we have previously described some of the effects of the opposite condition, that is *hypoconsciousness,* which is the most commonly observed state in man today.

HypsoConsciousness implies far more than a state of relaxation. Relaxation rather appears to be a natural consequence of a state of equilibrium. HypsoConsciousness means to attain a mature "I," one that is adult, stable and strong; an "I" of extraordinary firmness, capable of withstanding the anti-individual influence of the mass and the disintegrating effects of life "in the fast lane." The possession of this "I" does not imply leading a man to a "superman" state, but simply permitting him to attain the state of "human individual" attained by so few.

Below are some of the advantages to be obtained from an elevation of the level of consciousness:

1)   Self-control.

2) Voluntary relaxation.

3) A permanent and stable attitude of calm and tranquillity.

4) Full use and yield of the creative intelligence.

5) Improvement in health and increased vitality.

6) Increased working capacity with less fatigue.

7) Improvement in the capacity for adaptation and greater intellectual flexibility.

8) Liberation from perturbing ideas.

9) Isolation from negative environmental influences.

10) Retardation of the aging process.

11) Self-determination.

12) Voluntary use of the mind to achieve success.

13) Overcoming diverse complexes within certain limits.

14) Spiritual, moral and intellectual improvement.

15) Knowledge and attainment of a relative happiness.

To many people reading this list it may seem that relaxation or HypsoConsciousness is a sort of magical "elixir" or solution to one's problems. In successfully applying this system, however, it is essential to point out the importance of the "personal cerebral schema," that is, those patterns that are previously and profoundly recorded in the cerebral neurons.

An intense neurotic attitude of resistance is manifested in the form of a powerful, irrational and instinctive mistrust of the system of HypsoConsciousness, due to one's previous cerebral programming. This does not mean that it is essential to "demand faith to work miracles," like Jesus said, but that the prior existence of a genuine, profound desire to attain success in any endeavor should be there. Certain people, for example, possessed by a veritable instinct for self-destruction and motivated by a deep guilt complex, will of course find greater resistance in applying this method and should intensify their efforts if they are to overcome their inner barriers.

Certain personal traits favor success, while others curtail it. Favorable qualities are: dynamism, a positive mental attitude, a real and profound interest, an open and unprejudiced mind, a certain level of culture, an intense desire to master a technique, self-discipline, and a will to succeed and fight. The following characteristics are obstacles in the way of success: an inert personality, negativism, neurotic resistance, a weak will, mental laziness, a lack of intellectual curiosity, prejudices, an absence of an authentic desire for improvement and an incapacity for reflection and analysis. Logically it makes sense in the majority of people to adopt a more "favorable attitude" for the elevation of the level of consciousness.

As a system, HypsoConsciousness embraces the human being in an integral manner, relegating relaxation, at least in its orthodox sense, to second place by replacing it with a mechanism of total action that is far more profound; that is, the attainment of a high level of consciousness. Thus, it becomes more than an "anthropological physiotherapy" as Krapf defines relaxation. HypsoConsciousness, however, serves no purpose when the individual does not intimately desire to reach the goal he has set for himself because one cannot cure the patient who does not wish to get better. Free will in the form of an intimate individual desire is a factor of great force, the influence of which cannot be disregarded. The same treatment used to treat psychotic individuals in the field of psycho-neurosis cannot be applied towards the elevation of the level of consciousness which demands an ordered, volitive attitude.

HypsoConsciousness is a self-realization technique that demands an adequate persistent individual effort if it is to yield its fruit. However, it is advisable to obtain the direct help of an expert, whose chief aim is to aid the individual to overcome difficulties in understanding and to adapt certain aspects of the method to the individual's mentality. One cannot pigeon-hole anyone into rigid definitions that might offend deeply rooted patterns of behavior. Within certain established limits, it is advisable to follow each individual's personality traits. In other words, it is the work of the *skilled* person to find the appropriate motivation so that the integral comprehension of the method and correct practice of the exercises "penetrate" into the individual's psyche and are "accepted" by him as the necessary means to achieving what he is searching for. This does not in any way imply that the technique cannot be used by an isolated individual without the help of an *expert*, but rather that we recommend profound study of the theoretical precepts until correct understanding of them is reached.

When the exercises are practiced under the guidance of a specialist, they may be done in groups, with no more than fifteen people participating. When alone, on the contrary, one must practice them in a strictly individual way, without contact with relations or friends during the exercises, since other people become distracting elements.

Dr. Jacobson prescribes relaxation for the following disorders: acute muscular hypertension (nervousness); chronic neuro-muscular hypertension (neurasthenia); states of fatigue and exhaustion; weakness; pre- and post-operative conditions; toxic goiter; sleep disorders; hunger spasms; peptic ulcer; chronic lung tuberculosis; organic and functional heart disorders; high blood pressure; cyclothymic depressions; alcoholism; certain cephalgias and neuralgic pains; neurosis of the bladder; dismenorrhea.

On the other hand, Dr. Schultz prescribes relaxation for: hyper-intense emotions; nervous irritability and excitability; tics, stuttering, spasms and motor disorders; sleep disorders; spasms of the esophagus, pylorus, intestines, colitis; hypermotivity and hypersecretion of the stomach; heart disorders; high blood pressure; depressive states; drug addictions; headaches and rheumatic pains; neurosis of the bladder; dismenorrhea; bronchial asthma; pruritus.

I would like to underline the main differences between HypsoConsciousness and Schultz's autogenous, or self-generated training, which is somewhat similar. Of course, the main point of any relaxation technique must of necessity be an increase in the subject's consciousness. Jacobson's progressive relaxation aims precisely at the "consciousness raising" of diverse groups of muscles in order to obtain perfect volitive control over them. Schultz's concentrative self-realization begins with the same principle, with an awareness of certain natural bodily phenomena, such as weight and temperature. Schultz defines his system as a technique of self-hypnosis and he acknowledges that much of his inspiration comes from Oscar Vogt's work on hypnosis. Auto-suggestion plays an important part in his method. "We shall restrict ourselves to taking advantage of experiences, theory and practice of the autogenous treatment," says Schultz at one point in his work.

Even though I find autogenous training most effective and Schultz's research quite valid, I feel it is indispensable to point out a fundamental discrepancy between his theory of the level of consciousness and the one found in the system of HypsoConsciousness. I refer precisely to self-hypnosis. Apparently, within the framework of HypsoConsciousness, it is incorrect to consider autogenous or self-generated commutation as a process of self-hypnosis at least in the sense that is usually given to this term. Rather, commutation should be defined as a process of "de-hypnotization" because it produces an elevation of the level of consciousness. Here it is pertinent to ask if one is more asleep or awake during commutation. Based on my own experience and on the observation of other people's behavior, it appears that in reality, the subject elevates his conscious level during the process, and logically so, because by "becoming aware of his body," the individual is in a state of auto-consciousness that must necessarily be identified with the manifestation of the "I" which is invariably produced by HypsoConsciousness. Hypnosis, on the contrary, is a passing obliteration of the "I" with the consequent drop in the level of consciousness.

What Schultz defines as "attaining results inherent to suggestive states" is none other than the volitive influence exerted by the "I" upon the individual's imagination. Hypnosis, on the other hand, is the coercive influence of one individual over another person's imagination. Therefore, self-hypnosis is really an influence of the "I" over one's own subconscious. Generally speaking, the terms "self-suggestion" and "self-hypnosis" are incorrectly used because they in no way represent a state close to or similar to sleep, but rather indicate quite the contrary. When a person hypnotizes another person, the mechanism of sleep indeed exists.

One must be aware that the study of hypnosis is merely in its infancy and that even in this day, many so-called knowledgeable people consider it to be witchcraft. Its mechanism will not be known in depth as long as the mystery of sleep is not completely revealed. Hypnosis (when one is the subject) is a passive process, albeit an active one for the hypnotist. Suggestion is also a passive process for the person on the receiving end. On the contrary, self-hypnosis and self-suggestion, as both terms indicate, imply an active influence by the subject upon himself.

There is no reason why HypsoConsciousness should not produce the same or better results in the application of "self-treatment" of the disorders listed previously. Through intense observation of numerous students, I have discovered that many of them cured themselves of nervous asthma, palpitations, digestive disorders, nervous tics, high blood pressure, allergies, migraines, states of depression, chronic tiredness, insomnia, suicidal impulses, sexual neurasthenia, obsessive states and other such disorders. From yet another angle, I have satisfactorily observed how many maladjusted people who felt unhappy and discontented with life, finally learned to enjoy life to the fullest, thus achieving a favorable adaptation to society.

Due to the great number of consultations I have received on this subject, I shall give some scientific and philosophical considerations to the subject of Yoga and point out the differences between it and HypsoConsciousness. Many people ask whether HypsoConsciousness is based on Yoga, or whether it bears any relation to it at all. This question is of general interest, particularly since most people identify "Yoga" with relaxation.

Yoga is one of many Hindu philosophical systems and its mystic aim is union with God. Its doctrines were explained for the first time in Patanjali's _Aphorisms_ two centuries before Christ. Eight stages are differentiated on the path to beatitude: YAMA (self-control), NIYAMA (religious observation), ASANA (appropriate postures), PRANAYAMA (regulation of breathing), PRATYAHARA (domination of the feelings), DHRANA (firmness of mind), DHYANA (meditation) and SAMADHI (profound contemplation).

Yoga itself has been developed through various systems. Some give special attention to the physical body (HATHA YOGA). Others are more concerned with the mind (RAJA YOGA), and still others aim to channel the individual's emotional and devotional aspects towards divine adoration. Of course, Yoga is a mystical and esoteric doctrine, the main teachings of which are passed on in India through secret societies.

It seems plausible that Yoga, like the Persian, Chaldean, Chinese, Japanese, Assyrian, Greek, etc., esoteric traditions, originally sprung from some common source in Egyptian Hermetic Philosophy. Many Yoga "asanas" (postures) display remarkable similarities to those depicted in ancient Egyptian sculptures and engravings.

In *Techniques of Yoga*, Mircea Eliade says "there is probably no other oriental technique that demands such a difficult and prolonged initiation as Yoga... In the West, the essence of Yoga has been misunderstood and has lost significance and validity in proportion to the success it has been endowed with. The essential elements of the practice of Yoga cannot always be communicated in writing or even by simple oral teaching... There would be readers who, albeit unwittingly, would insist on carrying out certain exercises without control, thus running the risk of serious accidents. Non-supervised practice of rhythmic breathing has often caused considerable lung disorders." He later adds, "Yoga, the root of which is YUJ (to tie together), 'to keep tight,' 'to yoke together,' is a term used in general to denote an ascetic technique, a method of contemplation."

The mystical and ascetic aspects of Yoga are undeniable, because its theological aspect is closely linked to the theory of reincarnation. In fact, Yoga aspires to freedom from the pain that causes the human being an eternal future in successive reincarnations. Not to reincarnate, and to lose oneself in Nirvana forever, is the final aim of Yoga. To reach this stage one must free oneself from one's desires (which would cause reincarnation) and one must observe moral precepts and attain "the dissolution of the ego."

The philosophy of Yoga is correctly described in the _Bhagavad Gita_ (the Hindu sacred book with dialogues between Krishna and Arjuna): "Under this system, man neither hates nor desires... he is free from opposing pairs...he perceives that the senses move among objects of sensation....he situates all actions in the eternal, abandoning his attachment to things...he mentally renounces all actions...he is neither glad at obtaining what is pleasing to him nor sad at receiving what is disagreeable; he is capable of withstanding the force born of desire and passion...he is freed from hope and ambition...he is free of anxiety for all desirable things...he unreservedly abandons all desires born of the imagination," etc.

To analyze the true importance of Yoga and to appreciate its genuine value, it is necessary to discern some sociological differences between people of the East and West. Yoga is beneficial and suitable for the Hindu, because it not only offers him a religious orientation, it also promises the magnificent consolation of a better future existence in the life beyond this one. In short, the lives of many oriental people are considered by them as mere "preparation and brief transit towards death." The Hindu despises the material world for the sake of the abstract and his own philosophy has helped him to bear centuries of foreign domination, the strict subjection to the tyranny of the caste system, and the authority of the Maharajas. Consequently, Yoga for the Hindu is not only a mystic and religious discipline, but a necessary companion to their living conditions.

When analyzing the practical importance of Yoga for the West, it should be pointed out that there are remarkable psychological differences between Eastern and Western man. Eastern man despises life and is "in love" with death, that is, with the beyond. He despises the material world with all that it implies, including technological and scientific progress. His system of life, in which time is not important, allows him to devote himself without haste to meditation and the contemplation of the Supreme Being. This leads him to lose interest in the struggle for life, which is so important in the West.

Western man on the other hand, loves life and fears death. He tries therefore to get the best possible material advantage out of his life. Progress, economy, technology, science and time are all of extraordinary importance to him. He is not interested in dominating his desires. On the contrary, he stimulates them through the enjoyment of material commodities.

The practice of Hatha Yoga is most preferred in the West because it is restricted only to the control of the physical body without entering into moral or theological considerations. Schultz however, acknowledges that the numerous "asanas" are really a means of self-hypnosis, from which a stabilizing influence is derived. The main objections raised against Hatha Yoga concern the fact that it is a technique that requires years of practice to master, and that it is practically impossible after a certain age, since most of its postures demand the individual to be a consummate gymnast. In India, Hatha Yoga is learned from an early age in order to facilitate bone and muscle flexibility. Only under these circumstances can one finally master the technique. On the other hand, the enormous number of "asanas" in existence confirms the idea that Hatha Yoga is to be practiced for one's entire life dedicating many hours each day. In effect, it is said that there are as many postures as the number of species of living beings in the Universe. However, 84 main postures are acknowledged, of which 32 are usually practiced.

Hatha Yoga disregards the extremely important task of leading the individual to a higher integration of his personality through the comprehension of certain phenomena inherent to the human condition. Thus, in overall terms, Yoga is directed to the person's physical and emotional aspects, neglecting however, the intellectual one. It gives scant importance to the intellect other than what concerns mental concentration.

HypsoConsciousness has no relation to Yoga other than the shared desire of submitting oneself to discipline that enables self-control. However, all systems of self-control must of necessity share certain specific characteristics as far as the training of those areas to be mastered are concerned; those areas being part of the biological and psychic structure of all human beings. Therefore, both Yoga and HypsoConsciousness require mental concentration, but differ in their respective *modus operandi*.

HypsoConsciousness is essentially a system for Westerners. It does not lead the individual to a state of "awakened sleep," which would impede his earning a living, but on the contrary, enables him to attain a higher state of wakefulness. The state of "mental alertness" is therefore inseparable from this discipline. First and foremost, HypsoConsciousness attempts to broaden and sharpen the subject's field of consciousness, so that he perceives quality more clearly than intensity and volume. To become more conscious, to awaken, to shake oneself from the foggy lethargy of one's mental cobwebs are the goals of HypsoConsciousness.

The goal of Yoga on the other hand, is the

dissolution of the "ego"; the aim of HypsoConsciousness is to shape the "I." "To exist is to suffer," states Yoga; each action forms new "karmic circles" of cause and effect. In a way, Yoga seems to be a means of escapism; a means of fleeing from the reality of life to take refuge in the eternal sleep of "Nirvana."

HypsoConsciousness is eminently practical and achievable. It is clearly directed to the reasoning intellectual aspect of the individual, and above all strives to make the student understand the cause of his problems and attain an integral use of his creative intelligence. Therefore, one needs a certain intellectual training to use the technique. Nevertheless, it is often sufficient to have an alert and fully curious mind, for HypsoConsciousness teaches the individual "how to think" so that his judgment is in accordance with truth.

Perhaps the most important thing for the human being is the correct functioning of his mental faculties. "Nervous perturbation at the same time means mental perturbation" says Jacobson in his work. The yield of the intelligence - the functional capacity of the nervous system - depends to a great extent on the individual's emotional equilibrium. At the same time, the degree of correctness in the deliberate use of one's thoughts decidedly influences the nervous system. Perfection in thought is in practice the causal element of a correct emotional balance. In all truth, if the human being were able to exert a conscious and deliberate use of his mind, he would not suffer nervous breakdowns at all.

The exercises of HypsoConsciousness are mainly mental. The subject learns to control his imaginative states and to use them to his own advantage.

To sum up, the main differences between Yoga and HypsoConsciousness are as follows:

YOGA	HYPSOCONSCIOUSNESS
Is directed to the physical body.	Works chiefly on the mind and the emotions.
Seeks the dissolution of the "I."	Seeks the shaping of a fully grown and mature "I."
Is a mystic and ascetic discipline.	Is a psychological technique to be applied towards personal improvement.
Is an oriental technique designed for Orientals.	Has been specifically designed for Westerners.

EXERCISES FOR ELEVATING ONE'S LEVEL OF CONSCIOUSNESS

The exercises presented in this chapter address four basic aspects of the human mechanism which directly influence the maintaining of a low state of consciousness. They are directed at training the processes of breathing, imagination, vocalization and movement, and therefore, consist of four different groups of exercises, each of which shall be dealt with separately.

BREATHING

To breathe does not only means to supply the organism with the necessary fuel to maintain life, but also to delineate the schema of one's emotional, mental and nervous conditions. The respiratory and the nervous systems are equally influenced as far as excitability and inhibition are concerned. Similarly, one's emotional and imaginative states correspond to one's particular mode of breathing. There is no uniform breathing process for all people, as there are marked differences in volume and rhythm. Individual breathing habits greatly influence the various characteristics of one's personality, apart from representing the yardstick of one's physical and nervous vitality. A person who breathes deeply always has more psychic and biological energy. One who breathes shallowly is usually shy and asthenic. Correct breathing is one of the determining causes of good health, of a balanced nervous system, of a serene emotional state and of an alert mind.

Breathing is the flow of organic life. It is the only uninterrupted contact we maintain with Mother Nature, which, like an umbilical cord, supplies us with the elements necessary for our maintenance. The suspension of breathing means death. Moreover, the breathing process is the only vegetative function that can be influenced by our will. It is therefore the nexus between the cerebro-spinal nervous system and the vegetative system.

The training and mastering of breathing enables

one to extend one's volitive influence over emotional and nervous reactions that are normally beyond one's control. There is always an interaction between mental and emotional activity and the breathing process. During a state of emotional tranquility, breathing becomes more rhythmical, softer and slower; when one is tense, the flow of breath is halting, arrhythmical and shallow; after an emotional shock, breathing tends to stop or become almost convulsive; while concentrating, breathing becomes gentle and almost imperceptible; when the mind wanders, the breathing process becomes irregular.

The benefits of "respiratory re-education" are therefore both psychological and physiological. In order to appreciate the context of the different exercises which will be given, it is necessary to examine a few general points.

The adult usually breathes between 14 and 17 times a minute. Each time the thorax swells, there is inspiration and when it contracts, expiration. These two phases mobilize an average of 30 cubic inches of air in the lungs, so that the approximate volume of air breathed in and out in a minute is 2 gallons. This process, of air passing through the lungs in one minute, is called "lung ventilation." The maximum amount of air that can be expired after deep inspiration is the "vital capacity," the average of which is from 1 to 1.25 gallons. One cannot completely fill the lungs with fresh air, because a certain amount always remains in them, varying from 60 to 90 cubic inches that is not breathed out. The air that is not exhaled is called "residual air."

The breathing exercises presented below are not only designed for increasing one's vital capacity, but also have a direct influence on one's imaginative education and on one's ability to vocalize. In practice, the different groups of exercises are interrelated and mutually influence each other. Thus, breathing, speaking and movement, influence the imagination which are in turn influenced by it. Due to this, for example, certain breathing exercises are really designed to facilitate mental concentration, which would be classified as imaginative education. Because of this interrelationship, each exercise will be given a number and will later be re-grouped with regard to its goals.

COMPLETE BREATHING

A person normally breathes by filling only the upper part of his lungs. If he wishes to take in a large amount of air, his thorax swells considerably. This type of breathing is called thoracic breathing. The function of the diaphragm is not very important here. (The diaphragm is a wide muscle that separates the thorax from the abdomen and is used simply for breathing in.) When the individual breathes with his diaphragm, he increases the volume of air taken in and at the same time reduces the amount of residual air. Correct mastery of the use of the diaphragm allows one to improve the efficiency of the breathing process, which at the same time is one of the essential elements in effective speaking.

Most people truly suffer from respiratory insufficiency, a fact that may be verified by the following test exercise. Sitting comfortably, place your thumbs on your waist above the pelvic bones, so that your other fingers are placed backwards following your waistline until they touch each other at the back. You should breathe normally in this position and observe whether there is a swelling of the lower back muscles. If there is no swelling of these muscles, then your breathing is deficient.

Exercise No. 1 Complete Breathing
(Figures 1, 2 and 3)

Stand up, with your feet a little apart, your head upright and your shoulders back. Start to breath in while filling your abdomen, that is, projecting it forwards quite firmly until it bulges slightly. Keep breathing in until you have filled your lungs, now dilating your thorax, so that the abdomen is now naturally flattened. When breathing out, you should try to contract the abdomen gently in order to facilitate the elimination of the residual air.

In order to observe how the diaphragm works, lie down on your back and breathe a few minutes in this position. You must breathe without dilating your thorax and without moving your shoulders, thus swelling out the central part of your body.

This is an exercise for the re-education of breathing habits and acts as a basis for other, more complex exercises. It may be done as often as you please each day until it becomes your habitual mode of breathing, which is of course most desirable.

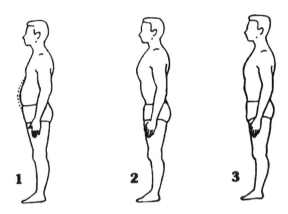

Exercise No. 2 Morning Breathing
(Figures 4, 5, 6, 7 and 8)

In this exercise, breathing and movement which are equally important, are combined. Its aim is to elevate your mental state, raise your level of consciousness, accumulate energy for the day, and produce an harmonious and balanced psychic state. The movements should be executed exactly as indicated, for each position creates a particular psychic state.

For greater clarity, this exercise will be divided into five parts, illustrated in the following diagrams:

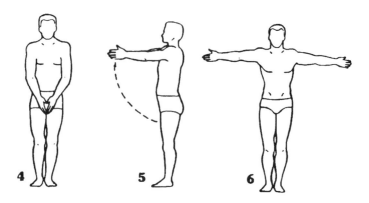

Stage 1: Stand, with eyes closed, heals together, toes apart,
spine straight, chin raised. With your arms held
out very straight, join the palms of your hands in
front of you at the level of your stomach. Your
finger-tips should touch each other.

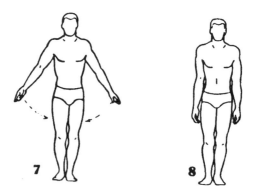

Stage 2: Start breathing in *through your nose*, gently pushing your stomach out and gradually raising both arms as you breathe, until your thumbs are at shoulder level.

Stage 3: Continue the movement, opening your arms outwards until they are fully extended and a little behind you, this being the moment when your lungs should be completely filled.

Stage 4: Start breathing out through your mouth and at the same time, lowering your arms gently as you breathe out, until the palms of your hands touch the sides of your legs. In this position you should have totally emptied your lungs.

Stage 5: Pause for a rest before repeating the entire exercise from the beginning.

It is essential that you execute the movements perfectly while thinking only of what you are doing. You must also synchronize your breathing so that the total filling up of your lungs coincides with the end of the third stage, that is with the end of the movement of your arms stretched out on each side. Breathing out should also coincide with the end of the fourth stage.

The whole exercise should last about 10 minutes, with a total of approximately 20 complete respirations. You must breathe in through your nose and out through your mouth, gently blowing out the air through half-open lips, as if you were whistling. This method may be changed on cold winter days to breathe out through your nose, so that nasal mucous does not become too cold through the lack of warm air, since you breathe in cold air and breath it out warm.

For people who are not in the habit of doing breathing exercises, the initial exercise time may be reduced to 5 minutes, but should be progressively increased.

It should be carried out standing up, preferably on an empty stomach before breakfast. It is important that it should not, under any circumstances, become an unpleasant duty. You should try to get a pleasant feeling out of it. In practice, a feeling of well-being arises spontaneously as you begin to notice an increase in vitality that helps you enjoy your daily activity. If you wish, you may also repeat it at night, as an aid to replenish the expenditure of vitality lost through work.

RELAXATION THROUGH RESPIRATION

Breathing in and out signals the flow of organic life. When one breathes in one becomes tense and alert and when one breathes out, one relaxes. During each day, people pass through moments of tension and relaxation. With conscious attention, a state of relaxation can be produced through the respirational flow.

Exercise No. 3   Breathing for Relaxation

Sitting or lying down comfortably with your eyes closed, fill your lungs with air, holding it in for a few seconds. Start breathing out gently and slowly through your mouth, as if you were blowing and trying to lengthen the exhalation process as long as possible. You must keep breathing out at this slow pace until your lungs are empty. Then rest and repeat the process as many times as you wish.

To get the best results, make sure that your breathing is as gentle and slow as possible. Due to its simplicity, this exercise is highly recommended for people with difficulties in concentration or in understanding other more complex exercises. It may be repeated as often as you wish during the day.

CONSCIOUS BREATHING

Breathing consciously induces a totally different psychic state from the normal one in which we breathe involuntarily. By being aware of the in and out flow of air, the individual establishes a connection between his will and his autonomic nervous system, thereby attaining self-control. Breathing is the switch that connects or disconnects one's nervous system and one's emotions and which enables the individual to modify his psychological and emotional states. Also an elevation of one's consciousness is produced, with the advantages already mentioned.

Exercise No. 4. Imperceptible Breathing

Either standing, sitting or lying down, start to breathe and "feel" the flow of air, while sensing the rise and fall of your chest. Feel how your lungs inflate and deflate, like a balloon. Continue until you feel identified with the rhythm of your breathing. Now, try to reduce the rate of your breathing until it becomes almost imperceptible and silent. Continue until you manage to relax completely or change your mental and emotional state. This exercise may be used at any time during the day when you wish to relax or attain a state of psychic ease. It is also recommended for people who suffer from insomnia to help them get to sleep. Remember that whenever one breathes consciously, as in the case of imperceptible breathing, one increases one's capacity for self-control.

All the breathing exercises indicated generally tend to raise the level of one's consciousness, to vitalize the nervous system and induce a state of relaxation, equilibrium, and tranquility. Respiratory control is vitally important for self-control because it enables one to quickly change states of fear or anxiety for example, into calm and peaceful experiences. It is essential to accustom oneself to thinking that voluntarily breathing in a profound way signifies that one is imposing one's own will on the autonomic nervous system.

While it is true that elevating the level of consciousness in itself enables the individual to control himself perfectly and change his emotional and mental states at will, it is also a fact that this state of alertness may be beyond the reach of people who are not used to reasoning and intellectual discipline. The exercises dealing with the education of the imagination are generally more complex due to their abstract nature. Several breathing exercises will then be given that will seem almost mechanical, but should be perceived as preparation towards the final goal of volitive action upon the vegetative system by means of conscious volitive breathing. Therefore, it is not necessary to do all the exercises, but to chose those which best suit each person's character and personal problems. However, it is advisable to do Exercise No. 2, *Morning Breathing,* every day because it is equivalent to recharging one's battery before going into action.

These breathing exercises do not prevent states of nervous tension, but they do combat nervous problems when these arise. Conscious breathing is merely the connection one establishes with the vegetative system in order to impose one's will upon it. Nevertheless, modification of one's habitual mode of breathing tends to suppress certain problems of nervous tension once and for all. This modification concerns the increase in one's vital capacity as a result of deep breathing. Deep breathing with continual practice should become a habit, which brings about interesting changes in one's character and metabolism. An increase in one's vital capacity is attained by the constant practice of complete breathing, as explained in Exercise No. 1, *Complete Breathing*.

To sum up, breathing helps one to rapidly change one's psychic state in order to maintain a specific condition or to intensify one's powers of concentration. Whenever a person changes his breathing rhythm or frequency, he modifies his mental and emotional state. If along with breathing, the individual keeps a fixed idea in his mind, such as an idea of calmness, tranquility and relaxation, etc., he shall achieve better results. Breathing is the means by which one surpasses the influence of thoughts on the vegetative or autonomic nervous system.

If in a certain moment during the day one feels a state of uneasiness and nervousness in the presence of another person, the appropriate action would be to intensify diaphragmatic breathing while keeping the mind fixed upon the idea of calmness and tranquility.

EDUCATION OF THE IMAGINATION

The imagination has an extraordinary influence over one's emotional and nervous states, because its designs dictate the patterns of nervous tension and one's emotional and mental condition. It is a fact that all parts of the body tend to follow the imagination. If one imagines a probable unhappy event for example, all one's muscles, both voluntary and involuntary, become abnormally tense. A defense mechanism sets itself in motion and tries to prepare the person for escape or attack. The thoughts which habitually cross one's minds are foundation stones upon which one builds one's physical, mental and emotional life. Each thought leaves its mark, evoking an emotional state equivalent to its intensity and quality. If one watches a scene of violence at the cinema, one's muscles unconsciously tend to imitate the action being watched. Suppose an individual is watching a scene in which another person is running fast to escape the pursuit of a lion. Without realizing it, he moves his legs imperceptibly imitating what he sees. Unknowingly, he reproduces the muscular tensions observed in others. A person thus mimics the states of tension of all the individuals he encounters.

One of the most important characteristics of the imagination is a lack of volitive control over it. Often, it is not the individual who imagines, but the imagination that works by itself, regardless of the "I." The average man is incapable of regulating his imaginative flow and is obliged to think constantly, with all of his nervous energies involved with the imposing images that arise from the association of ideas.

The imagination along with other human faculties, can be educated and to a certain extent submitted to the mastery of the will. Nervous tension and relaxation, when they appear unconsciously, are generally the product of something that the individual imagined, whether they concern a past, present or future incident. It is not even necessary for a person to imagine something specific and well defined, because the human being most often "imagines sensations," that is, certain perceptions that take place on an unconscious level, take over his imagination and provoke a certain psychic state in him.

There are three basic types of imaginative activity: that which is carried out deliberately at the conscious level; that which seems to be conscious albeit non-deliberate; and that which is carried out unconsciously. The imagination encompasses all the individual's levels of consciousness, from the unconscious to the supraconscious (when this exists). Thus, when a person imagines, he does not know whether his state of consciousness corresponds to the subconscious or to the conscious. People are so indissolubly tied to their own thoughts that they have no means of observing themselves, unless their state of wakefulness is elevated.

One of the most harmful imaginative habits is letting one's mind wander, that is, daydreaming or of "building castles in the air." By continuing in this habit, the individual gradually removes himself from reality to the point that he confuses the real with the imaginary. At the same time, he becomes "unconscious" because of the projection of his "I," and is therefore open to all kinds of negative influences that may penetrate his mind.

EXPERIMENTS RELATED TO THE IMAGINATION

The following two experiments present practical demonstration of the principles of "ideoplasia" (the effect of ideas on the physiological processes).

Experiment A

Make a rudimentary pendulum with a piece of thread or thin string and tie a ring or a key to it. The thread should be approximately 15 inches long. Then sit at a table and put your elbows upon it, so that the palms of your hands are joined at chin level. Hold the improvised pendulum by the thread so that the weight is hanging between the middle fingers of both hands with finger-tips joined, as indicated in Figure 9.

9

Now, try to keep the pendulum immobile, with eyes open, imagine that the pendulum begins to swing back and forth, towards and away from your body. You must intently wish the pendulum to swing. After a few minutes, you will discover that the pendulum in fact begins to swing in the direction you imagined.

Now change the direction imagining that the pendulum is swinging from left to right, that is, from elbow to elbow, and the pendulum will begin to move accordingly.

QUESTION: Why does the pendulum move?

ANSWER: The movement of the pendulum follows the direction of the experimenter's imagination showing that he made slight unconscious movements with his fingers to give form to the image that existed in his mind.

Experiment B

Sit comfortably. Close your eyes and imagine clearly that you are standing beside a railway. Imagine that a train is approaching from the left and passes in front of you, disappearing to the right. Try to imaginatively visualize the passing of the train from left to right. During this experiment, observe what happens to your eyeballs, which despite the fact that your eyelids are closed, will move and follow the direction of the train.

QUESTION: What is revealed by the fact that the eyeballs move in the imagined direction?

ANSWER: The movement of the eyeballs shows that there is a close relationship between thought and eye movements. The eyeballs always tend to move according to what one imagines. If instead of imagining a horizontal movement you had imagined a rocket taking off vertically, your eyes would have moved upwards.

Experiment B will be used to design a technique that enables one to relax. First, there exists an intimate relationship between imaginative activity and eye movements. Thus if a person manages to calm his imagination, his eyes will also be calmed, and conversely if he relaxes his eyes, his imagination will also reduce its activity.

Observation tells us that the eyes burn up a

high percentage of nervous energy. Both in work and in leisure, or during sleep, one's eyes are submitted to constant tension. Managing to relax them, means to induce a state of general relaxation, controlling the imagination and economizing one's energies. When the eyes are completely relaxed, one immediately stops imaginative visualization. Therefore the eyes can be regarded as the instrument the human being possesses to control his imagination.

Normally, when the eyes are at rest, they are in a relaxed state that can be called "vision into the infinite." In this position, the eyes look into space. In practice, this ideal posture hardly ever occurs due to one's ceaseless visual activity. When one looks at things, the eye muscles become tense and it is hard to relax them. When the eyes are at rest, a remarkable state of general well-being can be noticed, similar to that special psychic state brought on by standing on the seashore looking at the horizon. This looking into the distance produces a state of relaxation of the eyes, that in turn brings about a total state of relaxation in the individual.

Exercise No. 5
General Relaxation and Mastery of the Imagination

This exercise may be done with your eyes opened or closed, both at rest or during activity. It produces a state of physical and mental relaxation that lasts for as long as the exercise.

TECHNIQUE: Imagine you are looking backwards through your own brain as if your field of vision were inverted and turned backwards. You should NOT imagine that your eyes turn around in their sockets, but that they remain in their usual position, however looking backwards, just like a lantern that suddenly begins to shine backwards instead of forward. Do not attempt to exert any type of pressure or voluntary action on the eye muscles, for the process should be purely imaginative. You need not think that you can see anything special behind you, but merely imagine that you are looking backwards through your brain. Maintain this imaginative picture for as long as the exercise lasts. When you practice the exercise with your eyes open, you must keep your eyes looking forward without turning them sideways or fixing them on anything in particular. A variation of this exercise is to imagine that you are looking into space through solid objects, just as if your glance were lost in the distance without seeing anything. Both approaches produce the same effects and may be repeated as often as you wish during the day, lasting for a minimum of approximately two minutes. They can be extended according to your capacity for concentration.

It is of interest to note that this exercise produces a "parallel vision," that is, one that does not converge, which is precisely what provokes the desired state of relaxation of the eyes. In time, you should become accustomed to looking placidly and softly, without there being any violence in your vision. This technique may be used to attain mental repose and to expel negative ideas. It also serves as the foundation for attaining the state of "mental void," which will be introduced further on.

MENTAL CONCENTRATION

Mental concentration can be defined as the capacity to focus one's attention on one thing only, to the exclusion of everything else. Usually, one is only able to concentrate on those things which particularly interest one and even then, it is hard to concentrate in a sustained manner. Contrary to what is believed, intense concentration on a particular task does not imply using up more energy, rather it tends to reduce the use of it. Generally, when a person wishes to save energy, he does his work reluctantly, thinking that this lesser effort means less use of energy. However, he does not stop to think that the lack of enthusiasm causes the simultaneous existence of two extreme and opposed attitudes: the inner wish not to work and the vital need to do so.

Nervous tension always requires that there be the action of opposed forces which bring about the division of one's psycho-physical structure. When the union of the psycho-physical structure is perfect, the individual enjoys greater self-control and avoids the waste of energy that inevitably results from projecting one's attention onto several matters at once. Worrying also considerably undermines one's organic defenses, creating a state of nervous tension and making the individual work "at full steam." Undeniably, everything towards which one directs one's attention becomes something that "worries" that person to a greater or lesser extent. If one's attention is fixed simultaneously on many things, (as in the case of Charles who was mentioned in the chapter on "Real

Existence and Fanciful Existence") the level of "worry" is considerably increased. Many of the perceptions that one usually takes in, even if they are of the subliminal type, represent problems for the person, that is, stimuli that impel one to draw conclusions, make decisions or assume special psychological stances. It is possible that an incident witnessed in the street, although it may not directly concern one, provokes intense subconscious activity in one's mind, which is specifically designed to satisfy something that unconsciously worries one. For example, suppose that an individual fleetingly perceives an alarming newspaper headline about a possible threat of war in a certain part of the world. It is probable that his subconscious, terrified at such a prospect, may immediately begin to make plans for protection in the face of such an event. For the unconscious, this is a problem that is left pending, which must in some way be solved, and it will perhaps continue to worry the unconscious for a long time, particularly if it gets news of other similar events. This is only one of the many types of perceptions people receive during any normal day. In addition, there are also those perceptions stocked in people's memory that readily rise to the surface of ordinary consciousness when one lacks a certain capacity for concentration.

The more things an individual has to concentrate on at any given moment, the more divided his "I" will be, so that a high level of consciousness which is characterized by the manifestation of an indivisible, integral and mature "I," becomes impossible.

There are many degrees of mental concentration that are equivalent to different states of intensity of attention. Regardless of this gradation, which does not concern us for the moment, two basic states of mental concentration can be differentiated: tense concentration and placid concentration. Both may be either voluntary or involuntary. It is voluntary when there is a deliberate wish to fix one's attention on something to the exclusion of everything else, and it is involuntary when the mind is firmly captivated by a certain stimulus. We shall be concerned only with voluntary concentration.

Voluntary concentration is tense when accompanied by a muscular effort to "maintain" and intensify a mental image which may concern something abstract or concrete. To concentrate, one often resorts to tensing facial muscles such as frowning, clenching the jaw, and so forth, thereby creating a state of nervous tension.

So far, we have considered tension in its pathological sense, that is, as "exaggerated tension," analyzing the damage it can cause. However, it was stated previously that states of tension are both natural and necessary for an active life. Tension is only harmful when it becomes an exaggerated effort. Intellectually speaking, the general human problem is of a type that is essentially opposed to the phenomenon of nervous tension. In this case, we should speak of "pathological atony." In fact, mental concentration shall be defined as a state of imaginative tension, and mental dispersion as imaginative atony. One should not, however, confuse "pure" imaginative tension with states of emotional anxiety that lead to the type of anguished thought displayed by extreme tension. In this case, an involuntary concentration is produced and the "I" is ignored. Voluntary concentration is always a deliberate act of the "I." Intellectual atony is really a deficient manifestation of conscious thought with a predomination of subconscious activity, so that it is fundamentally an atony of the "I."

The chief objective of HypsoConsciousness, as

its name indicates, is to attain an elevation of the level of consciousness. This elevation is what we achieve through fortifying the "I," thus stimulating its consequent growth and total maturity. Concentration notably elevates the individual's mental tone and enables him to exercise his will and creative thought freely and completely.

Jean Claude Filloux, in his book, _Mental Tone_, states, "Will power, courage, perseverance, self-control and impassive calm in the face of adversity evoke in the human being energetic states of a particularly high tone. Reciprocally, the tone is particularly low in the case of passive, inert and agitated individuals who uselessly squander their energy; asthenics of all kinds, anxious, indecisive or impotent individuals; in sum, all those who appear destined to be toys of external forces, instead of voluntarily asserting themselves and actively adapting to the world leaving their own mark on it..." "For example, the persevering individual has tone because he knows how to use his strengths; the unstable and impulsive individual lacks it because he misuses his strengths or controls them wrongly."

Perhaps, the lack of mental tone is "a weakness of the conscious mind" due to a low level of awakeness, and of course to deficient training which co-exists with low states of consciousness.

As far as concentration and the wasting of energy are concerned, it is often argued that it is impossible to economize energies by striving for a higher degree of concentration because it implies a greater effort. In all truth, there is no greater effort required for placid concentration, only a tranquil maintenance of the mental image. On the other hand, concentration that is accompanied by great nervous effort undoubtedly causes a greater expenditure of energy, particularly when it is involuntary and motivated by a sudden and intense emotional impact.

Speaking of concentration, one must also consider the problem that concerns "deconcentration," that is, the difficulty of taking one's mind off certain ideas, experiences, events or perceptions that have occurred in the near or distant past. A complex is defined by an inability to "deconcentrate" the mind from an emotional impact or impacts in the past which are thus felt to be part of the present moment.

Concentration is not a tiring activity but one which represents the tone that should be habitual in the human being. When the mind wanders, a state of mental "hypotony" exists, and far from facilitating a rest for the mind, it actually causes a decrease in energy. On the contrary, it represents a multiplication of the factors already present in the mind, each one of which becomes an immeasurable problem in our brain demanding a solution.

The only truly effective state of mental rest is the one attained when one manages to "make one's mind blank," which is a state of mental void in which the flow of thought is temporarily suspended. This could be defined as total "deconcentration."

The technique for attaining mental concentration depends inevitably on adopting a special emotional and volitive attitude in which the person gives total, exclusive and absorbing importance to the activity, object or idea upon which he wishes to concentrate. It is a process of total voluntary indifference to everything that is not the object of interest. This voluntary indifference to other stimuli or ideas is the central key to the technique of concentration. One should, however, remember a very important point: *by concentrating properly, the individual manages to live in the present moment.*

The following situation will help to properly illustrate the mechanism of concentration.   A person concentrates far more easily when he is obliged to do so, that is, when there is a strong external pressure for him to fulfill a task or solve a particular problem within a certain time limit. Should there be some form of punishment for not fulfilling it within the specified time frame, the process of concentration will even be easier.

When a person wishes to concentrate on something, he should begin by assigning total priority to the matter upon which his attention is to be fixed. He must think that it is absolutely necessary for him to attend to the object of his interest exclusively, and that the focus upon this object is a "matter of life or death." Then, following the rules for the use of breathing, he should take in a deep breath in order to impose his will to concentrate on the whole of his psycho-physical mechanism. In order to keep up his concentration, he should focus his attention by elevating his state of awareness. The state of concentration is really an elevation in alertness and awareness of his mind. On the contrary, the incapacity to concentrate is caused by mental sleep, that is, by a low level of consciousness. In order to concentrate efficiently, one must dispel tedium and mental sleep, taking each idea, activity and object as if it were experienced for the first time in one's life.

Geniuses (people whose minds are awake) share such extraordinary powers of observation that when contemplating any object, they manage to discover endless things of interest that for the rest of the world go unnoticed.

During the process of concentration, it is essential to put aside all impatience or concern for the passing of time. One must try as much as possible to be fully awake in the present moment and live the period of concentration second by second.

Exercise No. 6   Mental Concentration 1

Take any object; place it on a table and observe it closely for three to five minutes until you perceive all its details. There must be no haste or worry about how long the exercise takes. You should rather be absorbed in the contemplation of the object. After having observed it, close your eyes and try to reproduce it in your imagination as accurately as possible. Open your eyes and now compare the degree of likeness that you attained mentally with the actual object before you.

It is advisable to change objects in order to faithfully reproduce their images if this exercise is done over a period of time.

Exercise No. 7   Mental Concentration 2

Sitting or lying down, close your eyes and concentrate your attention intensely and continuously on the different areas of your body, beginning with the smaller areas, such as your left thumb for example. Concentration should last for three to five minutes until you really manage to locate your "I" in the chosen spot which is to be recognized by the subjective sensation of "I am here."

As a means to perfecting the exercises already mentioned, it is recommended that you prolong the periods of concentration at will, persisting until you achieve accurate retention of the sensation.

The chief enemies of concentration are sleep or mental drowsiness, lack of the volitive decision to concentrate, lack of interest, and impatience.

Fundamentally, any process of concentration is "a patient, imaginative fixation" that is carried out deliberately.

THE CONCEPT OF THE MENTAL VOID

As previously mentioned, the state of "mental void" is the only period in which the mind is totally at rest. This rest shall be defined as "a momentary paralysis of the thought process" that is attained voluntarily. There are times when an intense emotional shock brings on a complete state of void in a person's mind, so that for a while he becomes incapable of reacting to internal and external stimuli.

In such a circumstance, the shock produces an abrupt return to very early levels of integration and the individual seeks refuge in the depths of himself, temporarily suspending the contact between himself and the outer world. The mental void is indeed a suspension of contact between the exterior and oneself. By considering the effort required for an individual to maintain an external and internal relationship simultaneously, the benefits to be derived from a rest from thoughts can be easily understood. Apparently, sleep seems to be a rest period for both mind and body.

However, thought activity is not suspended during sleep; it merely changes its level from conscious to subconscious activity. As observed on our scale of consciousness, there are no changes in the human being's intellectual faculties while he is asleep, except for a diminishing of the level of consciousness with the consequent increase of his oneiric state.

It should not be forgotten that the subconscious mind is also part of one's brain and that therefore, while asleep, one's brain is just as active or even more so, than when awake. One's mind never rests; it only temporarily alludes reality during sleep. The state of mental void, when achieved properly, is a very profound process, because within certain limits, it encompasses conscious and unconscious imaginative activity.

The benefits of a voluntary mental void are remarkable whenever one effectively manages to paralyze the flow of thought. There are really several degrees of mental void and it is difficult to speak of an absolute void because basically, there is always a certain subconscious activity. The state one should try to reach resembles an absolute mental void. Of course this "blankness of mind" is reached in its most profound degree only through regular practice.

The exercises for imaginative education are in actuality "thought gymnastics," **Internal Sports**™, that enable the individual to attain his volitive control. They represent a "consciousness raising" of a higher type of cerebral activity. These exercises allow one to attain a certain control over one's thoughts in the same way as the deliberate exercising of a muscle group. Thus, the mental void exercise is a "sensitization of thought" activity that enables the person to appreciate changes in tone in his brain by thinking and by stopping thought. Bear in mind that the practice of "mental void" is the only possible and real way to relax the mind.

Although this exercise may seem somewhat exaggerated to the neophyte, the benefits that can be derived from it should not be taken lightly. The "mental void" offers the individual in his intellectual function the necessary alternation of activity and repose that is manifest in all living organisms. To a certain degree, the mental void represents a state of far deeper repose than that of sleep. In fact, when a person awakens each morning from sleep, an equivalent renewal of organic and mental energy has not necessarily been achieved. One's burden of experiences weighs too heavily on one's psyche and does not allow the individual to face life with the necessary intellectual freshness and vigor. Sleep renews one's physical energy and is to a certain extent a daily rebirth. The mind, on the other hand, due to its uninterrupted activity, will be just as weary or sick each morning as it may have been the day before.

The mental void offers the individual an effective renewal of his mind. Once the cognitive activity of the mind has slowed down, the individual is reborn; fresh, youthful and attentive. Of course, this enables one to attain greater efficiency at work and to eliminate "brain fog." One's mental state or tone is of the greatest importance in maintaining a young and healthy body. Depressing thoughts, for example, greatly influence one's resistance and biological equilibrium by slowly undermining them. One's capacity for physiological recovery is greatly influenced by a positive mental state and a strong desire to live. This can be observed by examining the physical and psychological condition of optimistic people for example after having undergone surgery. These people recover in far less time and have far better chances of survival than those with negative thoughts and a lack of interest in life.

To sum up, the effects of the mental void exercise not only concern the intellectual sphere by setting the mind at rest, but extend also to the individual's integral mechanism acting as a balancing and stabilizing factor of utmost importance. In reality the deliberate and effective creation of a mental void reduces the speed of organic and nervous expenditure and increases the efficiency and quality of the intellect by renewing and rejuvenating it. This will be discovered by those who practice the mental void assiduously.

Exercise No. 8   The Mental Void

In the experiment regarding the visualization of the train, the relationship that exists between the eyes and the imagination was discussed. The first step in attaining the mental void begins with the relaxation of the eyes. To master the technique of this exercise, it is advisable to approach it in three stages, as described in the following pages:

Stage 1:

Sitting comfortably or lying on your back, close your eyes and begin to focus your attention upon them. After a while, you will notice contractions and movements of your eyeballs and a tendency to blink continuously, despite the fact that your eyes are closed. By using your will power, you should try to stop the slight fluttering of your eyelids and the muscular tensions of all the nervous activity in both eyes and eyelids.

Stage 2:

Forget your eyes and fix your attention on your breathing, that is, feel each inhalation and exhalation, trying to identify with the slight movement of expansion and contraction of the thorax. Feel clearly the alternation of breathing in and out, in and out, in and out. You should NOT breathe deeply, but just normally.

Stage 3:

After a while, when you feel that you have reached perfect identification with your breathing, you should forget the respiration process and center your attention on the imaginative visualization of the color black, which should continue until it tends to vanish.

The whole exercise, in each stage, should be done in a state of total immobility, keeping the body as inert as possible. There is no recommended fixed period of time for each stage, because each individual should fit it with his capacity and results. Under no circumstances should you proceed to the next stage without having mastered the former. The third and last stage may be prolonged for as long as you consider suitable, and falling asleep while practicing it does not matter at all. Try however, to dispel sleep through your will power. If you feel sleepy, then the exercise has not been done properly, unless its aim was exclusively to fall asleep.

When one feels an extraordinary calm and mental clarity, it means that the practitioner is on the path and must therefore persist until he truly attains the mental void. When one achieves this control, one feels absolutely nothing. Perception is totally paralyzed. The sensation that most closely resembles what one feels in the mental void is that time has stopped and that the individual is "suspended" in the present moment, without time, movement or perception.

It is necessary to recall that there is never a total mental void because a certain amount of unconscious activity is maintained, albeit reduced to a minimum. Perhaps the most appropriate description for this state is a "maximum possible suspension of the flow of conscious and unconscious thought." Unfortunately, there are no words to describe the mental states of HypsoConsciousness, so new ones have had to be created and in many instances, the use of metaphors to clarify the functioning of a particular psychic mechanism.

Possibly at the beginning, the exercise of the mental void may modify your sleeping habits and shorten the hours of sleep. This should cause no alarm because should it occur, it is due to a better and more effective recovery of energies during sleep. As a result, you will not need as much sleep as you did before. Once you have truly mastered this exercise you will be able to determine its duration before you begin, so that you may automatically return to your normal state of consciousness once you have finished.

The division of this exercise into three stages

should be followed during the learning period. Once you have mastered the exercise, the three stages should become virtually fused into one.

MOTOR RE-EDUCATION

The human being's kinetic mobility is made up of three principal mechanisms: reflex actions, automatic movements and voluntary movements.

Reflex actions are constant responses to most physical stimuli. They are either acquired or learned and represent the most elementary form of neuro-muscular behavior. Automatisms are defined by Professor Dalla Nora in _Biological Conditions of the Personality_ as "an ordered, but weak series of innate movements (emotional or instinctive imitations) or acquired ones (movements related to one's job, for example) that are summoned and specified one after another." Voluntary movements are those which are always accompanied by conscious will. They may be spontaneous, learned or applied. Whatever the individual's form of expression may be (reflex, automatic or voluntary), it is indissolubly tied up with emotional and mental states.

A state of terror for example, provokes a corresponding form of motor response quite different to that reflected by wrath, anxiety or placidity. There is a constant interaction between movements, emotions and thoughts and their interrelationship offers a fascinating possibility, which is to exert a certain mastery over oneself through the control of one's movements. This chapter will show that motor deliberation considerably elevates one's level of consciousness, which brings many advantages.

Only about half of one's voluntary movements can be truly called voluntary, because there is only a limited number of possible combinations of postures, almost all of which have already been mastered completely, and because they have been repeated countless times, they have become completely automatic. However before they became habitual, they must have been completely voluntary during the learning period.

A good example is the act of walking. When a

person walks, he is most often unconscious of what he is doing. If on a special occasion he has to walk in front of a group of spectators to demonstrate something, he suddenly becomes conscious of his gait and feels as though he were walking clumsily and incorrectly, even losing his balance as he proceeds. It is generally thought that automatisms increase the individual's productivity and diminish fatigue by mechanizing him. To explain this point, certain factors about fatigue need to be considered. In the daily activity of people who do not make any great, sustained muscular effort, muscular fatigue is very rare. What is more common is the sensation of tiredness and exhaustion, which shall be described as a state of "general fatigue." This fatigue should really be called "pseudo-fatigue," not because it does not really exist, but because it is often motivated merely by a temporary or chronic loss of one's normal mental tone. This general fatigue is usually accompanied by anxiety, irritability, depression, fear, melancholy and a lack of initiative. In order to clarify this concept, we shall speak of general fatigue and muscular fatigue. The former has already been defined, and muscular fatigue needs no explanation, for it is well known to all.

Despite the general consensus as to its

plausibility, the premise that automatisms "diminish fatigue and ensure personal yield" seems somewhat exaggerated. It may perhaps be effective only in a low percentage of tasks done in certain specific conditions, and only as far as performance and perfection in automatized manual tasks are concerned. For example, take a worker on an assembly line in a car factory whose job is merely to screw certain rivets into place. Most likely, if he started to think about how to screw in the rivets and tried to do it voluntarily, he would lose his usual skill, his productivity would diminish, and at the same time he would need constant attention and vigilance.

The problem is not quite so clear as far as fatigue is concerned, because what is economized in muscular expenditure may be squandered a hundred-fold in nervous and mental conflicts due to the low level of awakeness caused by automatic activity. The constant repetition of the same task leaves most of the mind free, so that it logically works actively on its own, while the individual is carrying out his tasks. Undoubtedly, this produces extreme dissociation between thought and action. This separation causes two currents of activity to co-exist, but in the way that the abstract and the concrete, the psychic and the somatic are opposed to each other. Therefore these two currents, despite being indissolubly united, act in opposed and different worlds. In other words, the individual is torn between two opposed tendencies: the manual work he is doing and the intense imaginative activity he develops, which is often far more desirable than his physical activity. On the other hand, his monotonous work is stripped of any type of motivation other than economic recompense. He thus works because he is obliged to do so, but he cannot help thinking that he is fulfilling a necessary duty. Basically, imaginative activity follows two different courses: the evasive and the acquisitive. The individual is concerned with how to avoid certain situations and how to attain others. Hedonism plays an important motivating factor. Desire appears as one of the most important elements in the imaginative game. Thus, there exists two equally powerful and important factors in clear opposition to each other: duty (work) and desire (the imaginative current). This counter position reinforces the process of dissociation between thought and movement, so that the mental and volitive tone drops considerably, and the individual's "I" cannot manifest itself. As a result of all this, the individual feels tired, perhaps more so than the apprentice who must still work "voluntarily."

Mental tedium and boredom are inseparable from states of asthenia and are reinforced by the lack of conscious volition. If a workman's daily activity were varied with moments to which he had to totally apply his conscious attention, he would certainly maintain a better physical and psychological state.

Automatisms provoke, reinforce and maintain a low level of consciousness. They cause general fatigue by breaking individual unity and by allowing the unbridled action of unconscious tendencies. In sum, automatic movements hinder self-control and a higher level of consciousness, favoring a state of mental drowsiness that is opposed to effective intellectual and energetic yield. Any voluntary movement tends, through constant repetition, to become automatic. This is unavoidable, but a person can stop automatic movements from totally dominating him. Otherwise, one runs the risk of carrying out an act of a man, not of "MAN," as Professor Dalla Nora puts it.

However, through vigilant attention, it is possible to re-introduce an element of consciousness into involuntary movements. This happens through moving deliberately, for example. In fact, deliberate movement reduces and helps one avoid states of general fatigue, while at the same time raising the level of consciousness and the volitive and mental tone. Voluntary movement through space creates, as a consequence, a state of self-consciousness in which there is a continual notion and consciousness of one's identity, that is, of one's "I." The individual locates himself psychically in his "I" and can successfully withstand negative impulses, inner conflicts and the harmful effects of heterosuggestion. In other words, from being an anti-individual, he now becomes an individual.

Through deliberate movement, it is possible to control states of nervous tension, avoid physical and mental fatigue to a great extent, control emotional manifestations and specifically, LIVE IN THE REALITY OF THE PRESENT MOMENT. At the same time, notable changes of a permanent nature are produced in the individual's neuro-cerebral structure, thus enabling him to considerably increase his intellectual capacity, in yield, practice, and quality. Thinking with complete clarity (which only occurs in exceptional circumstances) becomes a simple matter for the individual who assiduously and constantly practices deliberate movements.

Three main stages are to be differentiated in any voluntary movement: determination or will, the movement itself, and the resultant modification of the act carried out. Movement is a recurrent circuit that originates in the brain and "returns" to the brain. Involuntary movements do not bring about any new behavior modification, but for the most part, reinforce the circuit that had been previously formed. According to the way in which a person moves, he establishes a positive or negative modification in his brain; it is positive when it induces a state of wakefulness and negative when it leads to sleep.

A certain quantity of conscious voluntary movements temporarily annuls motor automatisms, and therefore broadens the field of consciousness. The individual's automatic movements are part of his emotional and instinctive mimetic repertoire, which in turn are coexistent and demonstrative of the profound mechanisms of the integration of his personality. Voluntary movements to a certain extent also express the individual's psychological state. When one consciously modifies one's way of moving, one is really transforming his personality as well, through the destruction of certain automatisms and the creation of others. Of course, doing so demands a highly awakened and alert consciousness. States of anxiety, fear, emotional depression, shyness and other negative mechanisms, temporarily disappear while deliberate movements are being practiced. They disappear for good when they are carried out constantly and assiduously for a long period of time. Movements made in a state of higher consciousness also act upon the intellectual and energetic sphere, causing an extraordinary clarity of thought and reducing sleep and fatigue.

The technique itself consists of moving calmly and deliberately, with full consciousness of the movement being practiced as if it were necessary to think in order to move. By reducing the speed of the movements, you will experience a state of calm and tranquility that is a sign of having attained a state of inner equilibrium. It is advisable to begin your training by executing previously selected simple movements. These types of movements have their place and time and should be practiced only at certain times of the day for a limited duration only.

Before explaining how to execute certain movement exercises, the following example will show that a profound transformation can be created in the individual through conscious and deliberate movements.

EXPERIMENT A: Choose a moment at which you are particularly tired or sleepy. Begin by doing deliberate and conscious movements for about three minutes. You will notice a progressive disappearance of your tiredness or sleepiness. Perfect concentration on your movements is essential and you must execute them calmly without haste, making them as perfect and precise as possible.

Exercise No. 9   Conscious Movements

The purpose of all the techniques given are to aid the student of HypsoConsciousness to gain progressive mastery over his movements. To accomplish this mastery, instead of specifically designed movement exercises, the student will work with the very movements he does daily, these having the advantage of not requiring any particular moment of the day to practice.

Begin with the simplest; the act of walking. It is preferable to practice this technique while walking in the street for a distance of no less than three or four blocks. Over this distance, you should keep looking ahead and walk slower than your usual pace, with full consciousness of your movements as if it were necessary to think in order to move. You must clearly perceive the *motive* sensation of movement, feeling each and every movement. This exercise brings on relaxation, rest, a state of calm, and at the same time, permits energetic recovery.

Absolutely all movements can be consciously executed, so it would be superfluous to draw up a detailed list. Of these movements, it is advisable to pay the greatest possible attention to the movements of your hands, which are by the way the most frequent and abundant. Anything done with the hands can serve as a practice exercise. The central context of this technique lies in the deliberate effort for perfection in movement, while trying at the same time to execute it as slowly as possible. You don't necessarily have to think about each movement; it is sufficient to have an adequate kinetic perception of them. The difference between thinking about breathing and "feeling" its flow, is however, significant. It is possible to "feel" without thinking. When a person unexpectedly experiences breathing difficulties caused by a head cold for example, he can be thinking about other things, but remain constantly aware of his "sensation of breathing," thus he feels the breathing sensation without thinking about it.

It is advisable to begin by thinking about your movements until you attain the correct kinetic sensation which most often appears as the simple slowing down of the speed of your movements. After a period of constant practice, you will notice that your new voluntary way of moving in turn becomes automatic by virtue of it becoming a habit. This should not worry you because as a result of this change you will have set up within yourself a circuit of relaxation, self-control and awareness. To change your way of walking, for example, means to correct and change an automatism. In this way, you will be giving life to a new cerebral and neural circuit that will be fundamentally different to its forerunner; one that is born from conscious reflective learning and that therefore reinforces and broadens the individual's consciousness, unlike the previous circuit which was formed at such an early age that the subconscious was completely dominant. Thus, everything learned reflectively and consciously, whether it be a new element or a corrected mechanism, noticeably elevates the level of consciousness and forms new neural circuits, now endowed with the superior awareness offered by an original, conscious, volitive impulse.

Conscious manual work is the best psychotherapy, because it acts as a stabilizing element and has an unsuspected capacity for cerebral modification. It is not an exaggeration to say that the human being's cerebral development during his long period of evolution has gone hand in hand with his manual skill and that brain and manual skill mutually influence and develop each other. Consciousness of one's movements enables the individual to live perfectly in the present moment, that is, to lead a real existence without any projection into a world of fantasy. Thus, the oneiric state that remains in one's mind, despite the fact that one is awake, is to a great extent expelled by deliberate movements.

In summary, conscious movement allows the individual to raise his level of consciousness, to live in the real world of the present moment, to relax, to control himself and to bring his intellect to optimum yield, with an increase in mental clarity and tone. The technique lies in the perception of the kinetic sensation through the deliberate effort of perfecting one's movements, whatever they may be, accompanied by a reduction in their normal speed. If a person is used to moving slowly, this technique will be of no use because there will be no conscious deliberation.

The technique may be applied either generally or specifically. It is general when it is used daily for certain periods, without considering the problems of the moment. It is specific when used for the momentary solution of a certain conflict. For a shy individual to counteract his inhibition to undergo a social confrontation, it is recommended that he move slowly and deliberately to counteract this inhibition. It may also be used at moments when one wishes to enjoy special mental clarity or counteract fatigue. After a while, careful daily practice will form new circuits that will make up an intelligent structural formation of a permanent nature creating a conscious awakened attitude which becomes an integral part of one's personality.

Vocalization

In this chapter, certain particulars of the mechanism of the spoken word will be examined in as far as they concern the way in which the voice influences the level of consciousness and consequently, a person's mental, emotional and nervous state. To this end, modulation and pronunciation will be explored, excluding the correction of defects in timbre, tone and intensity of the voice. The focus here is to give certain general indications, not specific cases on how to achieve correct pronunciation and modulation. This chapter will be primarily concerned with finding a formula that will enable one to elevate his level of consciousness through speaking.

In simple terms, the spoken word is a sonorous materialization of one's ideas, so that they may be grasped and interpreted by other people. In order to express oneself, a person has to relate, order and classify ideas and concepts at great speed, almost simultaneously with his words.

The mechanical production of words is part of all the other types of mechanisms described in the preceding chapters. The word is an efferent impulse that is materialized in a sound which, when recurrent, produces an afferent modification. The quality and perfection of the spoken word influences the mind, by either confusing or clarifying it. The correct exposition and careful pronunciation of words favor order, clarity and the proliferation of ideas. On the other hand, carelessness in expression disturbs the correct functioning of thought. Furthermore, the timbre and tone of the voice considerably influence the nervous system of both the person speaking and the person listening. There are voices that set one's nerves on edge, and others which produce relaxation.

The first few exercises deal with the improvement of articulation. They should not be considered as relaxation techniques but as preparation for attaining vocal consciousness.

The first element we have to consider for good diction is, AIR. The pressure of the air must be constant and uniform, which is achieved through diaphragmatic breathing, Exercise No. 1, *Complete Breathing Exercise.*

The spoken word is produced during exhalation and it is this stage that must be prolonged and measured. To achieve this, three basic exercises that help to regulate and measure the air will be given.

A. When you breathe out, prolong the exhalation of the air. Through your nose, breathe in slowly, gently, profoundly, silently, and completely. Pause. In a regulated manner, breathe out through your nose slowly, gently and silently, prolonging the exhalation as long as possible.

B. Inhale in the same manner as the previous exercise. Pause. When you breathe out, forcefully exhale the air in spurts, until you have expelled all the air from that breath.

C. Breathe in through your nose gently and slowly. Pause. Breathe out through your mouth blowing intensely, prolonging the exhalation as long as possible.

Once you have obtained the correct pressure and management of the air, you must train the speech organs that are involved in articulation: the tongue, lips, jaw and the soft palate. Although there is also specific training for each one of these parts, the exercises below deal with the total mechanism of the spoken word.

Diction Exercises

A. Read without making a sound, but while moving your lips, tongue and jaw, as if you were reading aloud. You should exaggerate your movements in order to attain volitive control over your speaking. After a while, repeat this same exercise, exaggerating your movements, but this time reading aloud.

B. Speak aloud with a pencil between your teeth, trying to make the sound as clear and precise as possible.

C. Speak aloud on any subject, articulating exaggeratedly and pronouncing each syllable. Pronouncing each syllable consists of making a slight pause between one syllable and the next, so that each word gains clarity. The pauses are so brief as to produce a positive effect without anybody noticing that you are dragging your words.

D. Read tongue-twisters aloud, aiming at perfect pronunciation and modulation.

The correct execution of these exercises is fundamental to bringing consciousness to the voice. Consciousness of one's voice is a special way of speaking that brings with it all the benefits derived from a high level of consciousness as has already been explored in detail. Just as in former exercises, faithfully follow the instructions below.

Exercise No. 10   Vocal Consciousness

In order to attain a state of consciousness of your voice, you should fulfill three main requisites:

- Speak syllabically.
- Articulate correctly and consciously.
- "Feel" your articulation.

It has already been explained what speaking in syllables means and also what correct articulation consists of. To be conscious, means that it is necessary to change one's vocal automatism, replacing it with another one of a higher quality. "To feel" one's articulation means to bear in mind the kinetic perception of the speech apparatus, which can be achieved from the start by thinking or fixing one's attention on the movements of the mouth and lips.

These exercises may be executed any time one wishes to speak, whether it be in trivial conversation or in public speaking.

One may think that by articulating consciously, one will be distracted in working out one's ideas, disturbing the correct flow of thought. However, by practicing these exercises, the individual will observe to his surprise, that exactly the opposite occurs; the mind is cleared, ideas are better strung together and one's intellectual yield improves remarkably. The elevation of one's state of awareness "awakens" and clears out thought. These exercises are particularly recommended when one has to face intimidating people, or simply as a means to calm, relax and control oneself under any circumstance.

For public speaking, one should begin by thinking almost exclusively of one's articulation, disregarding what is being said at first. By proceeding in this way, one's mind will clear rapidly and ideas will flow with ease. The elevation of one's state of awakeness does not come about abruptly but gradually, so that it does not attain its maximum level until after three or four minutes of practice in voice consciousness. Further on, other uses of the spoken word to solve specific problems will be discussed.

Consciousness of the "I"

The consciousness of the "I" is an extremely complex phenomenon that may occur voluntarily as a result of the aforementioned exercises or else through the direct creation of the "notion" of the "I." Consciousness of the "I" means having a notion of one's own identity. This identity has nothing to do with the personality, the body, the intellect, or the emotions whatsoever. Neither is it a state of self-consciousness, despite the fact that it is based upon it; it is something far broader and more profound.

It is well known that during the daytime one has moments of being "conscious of self," (however few and far between) and periods of "*self-unconsciousness*." For example, the boss of an office, may suddenly call attention to one of the employees in front of his co-workers, so that the employee in question immediately feels uncomfortably conscious of himself. This causes him great uneasiness, usually accompanied by embarrassment, fear, frustration and the sensation of being ridiculed.

Remember what was said about the "I" in previous chapters: The "I" is what is the individual's own; the "we" is what is not his own . . . There is an "I" in all individuals, but it is usually kept outside of the functional mechanism of the intellect. Furthermore, it is not a mature, developed and adult "I," but a diminished, fragile and weak one. To discover what happened to the employee who was singled out and why he felt the way he did, the situation must be considered in detail. He had been working at his usual job with his "I" asleep and his "we" awake. He suddenly experienced the emotional shock of feeling himself observed by everybody and was reduced to passively accepting what was said to him. His "I," which was asleep, suddenly woke up, as any emotional impact "shakes" one from the state of habitual sleep, and displaced the "we" from his field of consciousness. At that moment, the individual "saw himself" clearly, that is, he brusquely and fleetingly glimpsed the subconscious structure of the "we," and identified with it, thus feeling like an impotent child (the subconscious), naked and ashamed. His mask was dropped and he felt that he saw himself and was seen as he really was and not as he appeared to be. (The word *person*, from *personality*, comes from the Greek *prosopon* which was used to denote a theatrical mask).

The "I" is covered by the dense blanket of the personality which will not allow an individual to know himself, that is, to know his "I." It is well known that when a person integrates into a crowd, his behavior becomes far more spontaneous and demonstrative than when he is alone. It is pleasant to know and deal with people who behave and react spontaneously because they seem more human and cordial. However, we cannot ignore the fact that spontaneity is a product of a well organized automation. The individual only reacts "spontaneously" in his relationships when his social automatisms are functioning perfectly. If he has to approach a subject that is not "automatically" integrated within him, he will assuredly lose his spontaneity. On the animal scale, the human being is the least spontaneous and it is precisely his conscious reflective quality that differentiates him from animals. Animals and children are totally spontaneous without of course, this implying human quality or faculty. What is usually considered as spontaneity or "fluidity" is exactly the opposite, because in practice, it represents a false spontaneity of a compulsive nature that is but a mere product of the prevailing automatisms. True naturalness in dealing with people and in one's emotional reactions in relationships is learned and is not spontaneous. Due to this, it is inevitable that during the first period of training, the states of consciousness of the "I" coincide with a certain lack of naturalness, for the individual is learning a new way of behaving, thinking and reacting. Thus, self-consciousness robs the individual of a certain naturalness if he is not accustomed to being aware of himself and acting with his "I" instead of his personality. Consciousness of the "I" is not something that may be practiced indiscriminately by everybody, because only those who profoundly desire to exist as true individuals have access to it.

Consciousness of the "I" is the psychic identification of the individual with his "I," which is the point of union between past and future. It signifies "rejecting identification" with perceptions, emotions and ideas that do not have the true "I" as a point of reference. This has nothing to do with selfishness, since it is a mental phenomenon that has no relation to emotional or instinctive considerations. The "I" spoken about here is not the one that possessively says, "I want that car," "I want to eat fruit" or "I want to smoke a cigarette." It is not even the "I" that says, "I am desperate" or "I am happy." The "I" is a pure, abstract intelligence that observes, knows, analyzes and judges.

A person cannot be selfish if his intelligence is directed by truly conscious and intelligent formations that are stripped of the instinct for possession that prevails in the habitual structure of the personality. Of course, the word egoism is used incorrectly if one considers the true significance of the "I." The individual who is truly selfish is the one who does not exist as an individual, but as an "anti-individual," because all his desires are destined to satisfy needs of a compulsive nature and to feed a false ego that, like an insatiable idol, demands blind adoration and the sacrifice of human essence.

Normally, an individual identifies with all the things that enter his field of attention, particularly when they impress him intensely. Logically, these identifications bring about a loss of self-consciousness. Thus, any unpleasant incident becomes a disturbing element to the observer, due to identification which is a projection of the "I." In such a case, the observer unwittingly transforms the spectator into the actor, despite not having participated actively in the matter. The "I" is the knower, the thinker, and should always be maintained in this way, because when lost, it is no longer an "I," but a "we."

Consider this interesting fact that may shed much light on the phenomenon of identification. Psychically speaking, the most significant difference between the state of sleep and that of being awake is that when the individual is awake, he maintains to a certain extent his capacity to detach himself from his imaginative activity, to observe and analyze it. On the other hand, when he is asleep, the individual totally loses his status as spectator of his own imaginative kaleidoscope and becomes directly involved as an actor. This fully coincides with the theory of the levels of consciousness spoken about here, because if a person were totally awake he could control, direct, and observe his own imaginative behavior, and this does not happen in practice. It is precisely during the daytime while in a state of apparent wakefulness that the individual constantly loses his status as observer, becoming emotionally involved in matters that do not directly concern him. This change from observer to actor comes about simply by the projection of the "I." Thus, sleep should be defined as a projection of the "I" to the subconscious. The periods of sleep and wakefulness represent alternating projections of the "I," which are manifested in one's consciousness during the day (although not very strongly), and in the subconscious during sleep. To phrase it better, the "I" hardly manages to have even a brief glance at the real world, because its usual dwelling place is in the subconscious. The alternating projection of the "I" is what supplies the organism with an adequate homeostatic balance, by fluctuating from a state of excitability (awakeness) to one of stabilization and inhibition (sleep).

Some psychiatrists state that sleep is "a necessary escape from reality." It is perhaps more correct to say that sleep is a temporary obliteration of the "I," which is focused on the subconscious in order to support and fortify vegetative life which would probably deteriorate considerably without this assistance. Yet what happens to the child, who does not yet have an "I"? The impulsive force of the "I," that is, the dynamic energy that serves as a central structure for the formation of the "I," is creative sexual energy. Energy, not sex. The child thus possesses a purely libidinous "I," which is precisely what is projected to the subconscious or unconscious in order to fortify his weak organism. The child sleeps far more than an elderly person, whose organism has already worn out. The libido furnishes the bricks and mortar of the "I," which however, in its maturity has no more relation to instinctive energy than that which exists between the tree and the seed.

Consciousness of the "I" is acquired gradually through the correction of harmful habits. Among such habits, a prominent position is given to the habit of doing several things at once, and particularly that of projecting the "I" into the past, or the future, through imaginative "wandering." The individual should try to do everything in an orderly fashion, one thing after another, giving all his attention to the activity of the present moment. At the same time, he must separate exterior perceptions from his own "I." When watching a movie, for example, he must be fully aware of what he is doing and be able to perceive that "I am watching this movie." When discussing any subject of interest with another person, when watching an impressive event, when reading a book, eating, etc., he must have a clear notion of "I am doing this." In sum, it is a question of "not losing the "I," of not letting the notion of one's own identity escape oneself.

"Self-perception" should simultaneously be included with external perception where the individual places himself as a separate mental unity from the external world. The "I" must be here; the external, there. This is what it means to have a true notion of the "I." The following exercise helps to create the notion of the "I" and should be contemplated upon daily, for some time. This contemplation evokes a state of relaxation, firmness and tranquility, and it is a tool that helps to stimulate a state of consciousness of the "I" at will during the daytime.

Exercise No. 11　　Consciousness of the "I"

Place Fig.10, the diagram of the "I," on a table at about 25 inches from where you are sitting, so that you can observe it comfortably. Then join the middle finger and thumb of your left hand at the tips, and keep them in this position throughout the exercise. Next, breathe in deeply through the nose, exhaling slowly and gently through half-open lips.

Immediately fix your attention on the center of the figure, in which the word "I" is written, keeping your eyes concentrated on this spot for approximately three to five minutes. There is no reason to worry if you feel sleepy or actually fall asleep.

You can repeat this exercise as many times as you like during the day.

When you have practiced it for some time (minimum 30 days), you can try to voluntarily produce a state of consciousness of the "I" during the daytime without the figure in front of you, merely by joining your finger-tips as indicated above. This may be done at any moment, regardless of the activity you are engaged in, the sole condition being that your left hand be free. This exercise produces at will, rest, relaxation, calmness, firmness and an elevation of the level of consciousness.

Figure 10

USE OF THE REFLECTIVE POWER

One of the highest conquests a human being may aspire to is to achieve a complete integration and comprehensive behavior for himself. A large part of the structure of man's personality today is made up of "unconscious, non-intelligent" mechanisms, that are the result of conditioning, imitation and outside influence. The personality, as we know, is a mechanism designed to enable the individual to adjust to his environment. Unfortunately, this adjustment is not always "intelligent." Allport says, "... not all structures formed in the personality are intelligent configurations of it. Many of the structures are complex clichés and stereotyped habits, forced upon the individual who reacts through psychological means that are too subtle for him to deal with in a truly comprehensive way."

In reference to the integration of the personality

which is the organization of its diverse mechanisms into units of a higher order, Allport points out the partiality of the process:

"Many experiences (perhaps the majority) never manage to be integrated adequately: they occur; there is a period of adjustment and the matter then disappears and is forgotten. Assimilated experience does not go at the same pace as the individual's momentaneous and passing experience. We constantly encounter new events to which we must respond, yet when we respond, we do not always incorporate the action into the permanent structure of our personalities. We allow rather our former habits or our previously shaped attitudes and features to suffice and we do not bother to alter our integration to cover the new characters of the surrounding world or the new truth we have found. This fact is of enormous importance. It is well known that men direct their conduct by using inappropriate habits, stereotyped ideas and empty verbal symbols. Most people do not learn as much from their experience as they believe they do. There seems to be an inertia in the process of integration. A few conventional habits, a few fossils of ancestral political-economic beliefs, a handful of superstitions and a vocabulary of clichés satisfy most people. The rule seems to be that unless there is a strong desire to alter an unsatisfactory habit or feature, or unless the demands of the world are too insistent for us to continue using our former equipment, or else for some other reason an individual is truly malleable, with an open spirit, his personality will continue to make use of the rough, but ever ready resources upon which he already counts on to face up to the demands of life, and he will thus avoid the need to effect an integration."

Comprehension is indispensable for a person to be able to behave consciously. When this process does not exist, the individual is a veritable machine with stereotyped reactions and limited intelligence. Unfortunately, common man displays an extraordinary mental laziness that prevents him from meditating on his daily experiences. The lack of reflective comprehension is what marks the difference between the "anti-individual" and the individual. Habitual meditation, accompanied by the right state of consciousness, helps to develop the human being's higher faculties and more profoundly delineates his "human" status from the animal. Nevertheless, it should be pointed out that there is an enormous difference between mere thinking and conscious reflection. Everybody thinks, but only a few reason; of the few who reason, only a minority are conscious. Thought may exist without any logical reasoning and reasoning may exist without consciousness.

In its broadest sense, the reflective capacity leads to

true and accurate judgment only when it is accompanied by a high level of consciousness. When this is not the case, intellectual elaboration undergoes serious distortion due to the individual's latent oneiric state. Thus, a person may arrive at an erroneous conclusion despite having meditated profoundly on some matter because he lacks a higher level of consciousness. An example: a person is submitted to a simple problem three or four minutes after waking in the morning. In spite of possibly making considerable efforts to do so, he cannot find the solution as his mind is still drowsy. If a person had no experience of states of more heightened awakeness, his usual mental state may quite well be oneiric without him even realizing it, which is compatible with the theory of the degrees of awakeness. How can a person realize that he is half-asleep if he does not know any other higher state?

It does not matter how intelligent or cultured an individual may be; if his mind is perturbed by his oneiric condition, his conclusions regarding some of his problems will necessarily be at least partial and incomplete, if not erroneous. Sleep seriously distorts the process of intellectual elaboration, and is responsible for the human being's "mental poverty." In fact, it seems that the habitual mental state of most people is hazy and imprecise. Only in exceptional circumstances does the individual think with full clarity. With his mind in the shade, he is obliged to tirelessly seek the solution to the infinite number of problems he has to face in life. To this end, he thinks, thinks and thinks again, but does not consciously reflect. He does not know that because of his deficient intellectual functioning, he is missing out on the best things in life and is barring himself from a knowledge of the marvelous world of consciousness. Unfortunately, it will not suffice to tell a person this; he must understand it himself.

As far as personal problems are concerned, constant rumination over them generally contributes no new elements to what the person already knows. Besides, the emotional repercussion of difficulties considerably perturbs the intellectual process. It is well known how difficult it is to make the right decision when one is upset, anguished or afraid. Many people are true victims of their emotional compulsions, because of the permanent indecision caused by them. Remember that emotional behavior pertains to childish levels of integration, that is, to that period in which the subconscious prevailed. Prevalence of the conscious part over the subconscious always comes as a logical consequence of attaining a high level of consciousness. Thus, this elevation not only enables one to think regardless of perturbing emotional states, but also to think without the oneiric influence.

Below are two exercises that enable optimum intellectual yield and which may be applied to the solving of difficult problems that escape one's habitual mode of thought. By carrying them out carefully, they bring about an extraordinary state of mental clarity that surpasses the limits of common reasoning.

Both exercises to a great extent expel the "oneiric burden" that is common, elevating the level of consciousness temporarily, while the person in question attempts to find the sought after solution. Of course, all the exercises we have introduced elevate one's level of consciousness, but naturally with certain fluctuations during the day. The exercises below lead the intellect to a higher state of wakefulness far beyond that resulting from the daily practicing of the exercises. Really, their role is to momentarily intensify one's personal state of awakeness.

Exercise No. 12   Solving Problems

Move deliberately for three to five minutes, just as in Exercise No. 9, *Conscious Movements*. Then sit down and write out the problem by hand, thinking while you are doing so of the movements you are making with your hand and trying to write consciously and deliberately in your best handwriting. Defining or explaining the problem itself should be as brief and precise as possible. Next, after meditating, note down possible solutions in the same way as indicated above, finally trying to decide upon the one you consider the most appropriate.

Exercise No. 13   The Applied Use of the Intellect

Consciousness of the voice is used for this exercise, as in Exercise No. 10, *Vocal Consciousness.* In this case, it is a question of motivating conscious reasoning through the word. To this end, you should expound your problem aloud, as if you were explaining it to someone. When speaking, you should at all times fulfill the requirements for vocal consciousness, that is, pronouncing and modulating correctly, articulating each syllable and "feeling" your articulation. The reasoning process is continued in this way until you reach the desired solution. Your voice should be clear and expressed with a certain intensity. (This exercise offers the same advantages as the former exercise, but is also useful for keeping one's mind clear when arguing with other people or when one has to speak in public).

It should be pointed out that the constant and methodical practice of Exercise No. 9, that is, of *Conscious Movements*, will eventually bring about an interesting modification in one's cerebral circuits, thus incorporating into them, if one can term it as such, a "circuit of consciousness."

As stated in Chapter 12, if one practices deliberate movements, there comes a moment when these movements become automatic, but with the marked difference that they are "conscious automatisms" if this somewhat paradoxical term may be used. In fact, if one studies the question of conscious reflective learning, one will find that this is precisely what shapes the real "I." The "I" is shaped, fed and developed by that type of learning that is of a conscious reflective nature. Motor re-education consists of learning to move in new ways in order to build a renewed motive circuit. Once this is achieved, the individual permanently modifies his cerebral and intellectual mechanism because he has attained a higher state of consciousness.

Thus, motor re-education will in time constantly produce the same benefits in thought as those that can be temporarily achieved by doing Exercises No. 12, *Solving Problems*, and No. 13, *Applied Use of the Intellect.*

SUCCESS

One of the human being's basic needs is his desire to feel important and esteemed by others. He needs to be respected and needs to respect himself. Success in life is the much sought after reward that everyone pursues, but not all attain. Undoubtedly self-control is one of the most important pillars of success. The individual who knows how to control himself has an advantage over those who lack this ability. Nevertheless, this mastery must in some way govern the subconscious mind, because within it lies the hidden desire to fail (which is far more common than is usually thought), and the subconscious mind almost always hinders success.

Let's analyze what occurs in an individual's mind. Foremost in this discussion is the mechanism of the co-operation of the subconscious. When this co-operation is lacking, it is far more difficult to attain what one desires. One of the ways in which the subconscious influences the individual is by its ability to convince him that what is most often only a manifestation of unconscious activity usually ignored by the rational mind, is what is commonly called "good luck." It becomes necessary to get the subconscious interested in one's specific project until the individual manages to convince it of the need to accomplish that project. If a person manages to arouse the subconscious' interest, he will certainly manage to achieve his desires without too much difficulty. In order to utilize the subconscious, however, he must first consider that it is strongly influenced by fears, desires, and hidden frustrations which are often more powerful than one's conscious will. These inner resistances cannot be overcome simply with the common means within one's reach, so the individual must resort to intensifying his volitive action in some way on the subconscious, weakening its opposition at the same time. This is wholly achieved by the elevation of the level of one's consciousness.

Many people do not believe that the subconscious influences their lives so decisively and therefore, the following two examples are for their benefit.

Example No. 1:

A doctor in a hospital attended to a woman who had lost her sight. After several examinations, he arrived at the conclusion that her blindness was psychosomatic in origin. He began to treat her with hypnosis and learned that her husband frequently got drunk and during his drinking bouts, seriously abused her. Her subconscious reacted defensively by blinding her as an evasion from her problem. When her husband learned of the origin of her illness, he stopped drinking and began to treat her much better and take proper care of her. With the right hypnotic treatments, she finally recovered her sight.

Example No. 2:

A young man was given an electro-cardiogram. The doctor told him that he had a heart murmur and asked him to return for another examination a few days later. In the interim, the patient experienced serious symptoms, feeling strong palpitations, breathlessness and pains around his heart. At his next visit to the doctor, he was given a piece of amazing news: the EKG had been misinterpreted and the patient's heart was in perfect condition. The patient left relieved but his symptoms continued indefinitely because of the strong emotional impact caused by the supposed disorder.

These two cases show how the subconscious may cause serious disturbances, bringing on such extreme manifestations as blindness, paralysis or cardiac neurosis. The subconscious becomes actively mobilized by whatever makes a sufficiently intense impact on it.

There are two currents of desire in people: what is intimately desired (which is often ignored) and what is desired on the surface, which may be in a vague, weakly defined form. An individual often finds himself torn between contradictory impulses that naturally hinder his reaching pre-determined goals. Thus, he may strongly desire to own a car, but at the same time feel an intense, inner apprehension to drive it, perhaps fearing even an accident. Under these circumstances, it is not very probable that he will one day become the owner of a vehicle because he subconsciously rejects it.

Observe how the mechanism of subconscious desire acts. An individual may be firmly determined to attain economic success and, driven by this impulse, pursue a certain type of business. He plans carefully, works twelve hours a day, is neat and careful with the financing, but fails in the end due to a series of unexpected factors. This situation may repeat itself three or four times with variations until he finally gives up his attempt to do something important and becomes an employee with a low salary.

One must ask why this man cannot attain success? Does he lack the necessary intelligence and business sense? It is quite probable that not only did he lack the co-operation of his subconscious, but that his subconscious was also against him from the start. As this was something that takes place in his own mind, it lead him to make mistakes in the crucial decisions he had to make, without his realizing it, that is, he unconsciously desired to make mistakes and did so because he intimately wished to fail. What can lead a person to unconsciously seek failure? Some of the causes which are really difficult to evaluate are: Guilt Complex; Fear of Responsibility; Shyness; Oedipus or Electra Complex; Disorientation.

GUILT COMPLEX

A strong guilt complex can drive a person to gradual self-destruction through failure. Convinced of having committed certain unforgivable acts, he unconsciously seeks to expiate his guilt through suffering and punishes himself by denying himself the success he consciously desires so strongly.

FEAR OF RESPONSIBILITY

A man who fears responsibility is usually content to belong to the mass. Nevertheless if at a certain point, he is driven by pressing economic needs and takes up some important project, he may encounter many obstacles in his way. These of course are only a reflection of his own mental barriers.

SHYNESS

Shyness is similar to the fear of responsibility, with the difference that it may block the individual even more seriously by disturbing his social relationships which will of course deprive him of many opportunities.

OEDIPUS OR ELECTRA COMPLEX

The Oedipus complex (called the Electra Complex in women), creates a state of dependence on the mother image in men (and the father image in women), which frustrates and hinders the individual's capacity for accomplishment. The past co-exists with the present and the future within the subconscious. Subconsciously speaking, the situation still exists in the present for the man who fell in love with his mother when he was a child. He involuntarily seeks anything that tends to reinforce his union with the mother image and struggles stubbornly against anything that threatens to destroy it. Success, with all the circumstances it brings, is precisely a material and undeniable manifestation of the independence from one's parents. An individual with an Oedipus or Electra Complex may deny himself or herself success in life in order not to abandon the beloved parental image. This brief commentary only concerns the implications of this fixation for success, since its general effect is intricate and variable.

DISORIENTATION

The individual who does not know exactly what

he wants cannot be successful in life, because he is paralyzed in the face of many undefined desires.

Conclusion: Failure is basically a mental attitude; it lies within the person and not outside of him.

It is pitiful to observe skilled and intelligent individuals who have not been able to succeed because their minds were blocked by some of these compulsive elements. Suppressing them would mean destroying the dam that holds back and paralyzes thought. Of course, this is not the specific task of HypsoConsciousness but that of the therapist, counselor or psychiatrist. An elevation of one's level of consciousness does not destroy the neurotic formations of complexes in themselves, but inadvertently introduces into the subconscious an element of consciousness and reasoning, thus making it more aware, which ultimately leads to more intelligent and practical behavior. However, this strongly depends on the quality, continuity and constancy of practice, as likewise on each individual's mental attitude.

In general terms, any elevation of the level of

consciousness markedly facilitates success in life, because it mobilizes the resources of the whole mind and leads the intellect to high yield, thus facilitating the co-operation of the individual's subconscious in any enterprise he may choose to undertake. Regarding success, the great importance of personal qualities such as perseverance, the spirit of sacrifice and self-confidence cannot be ignored as well as the important role of deliberate and sustained enthusiasm which helps to keep the impulse for success alive.

It is also essential for the individual to carefully analyze himself until he is convinced that he really desires a particular thing and to analyze the advisability of the effective outcome of his project.

Exercises No. 12, *Solving Problems*, and No. 13, *Applied Use of the Intellect*, are recommended as an effective aid in planning and deciding methods of action.

GUIDELINES TO HELP PREVENT NERVOUS TENSION

Certain habits encourage states of nervous tension, while others help to prevent them. It is good to have a general idea of what should be avoided and what should be encouraged. Of course, these guidelines have the same limitations as any prohibition concerning habitual acts that have the power of an automatism. Nevertheless, just as with a stomach ailment, an individual should know what irritates his condition and what is good for it. With a little effort, a person may correct certain automatisms to replace them for other more beneficial ones by following the methods in this book. Some habits require only a little attention in order for them to no longer be harmful. It all depends on what the individual's primary concern is, because one cannot forget that each person organizes his life according to the goals he thinks are desirable to attain. Benjamin Franklin, for example, possessed by a strong desire for personal betterment, was able to overcome the serious defects he discovered in his character through a careful analysis of them.

Summed up in twelve points are the personal qualities which endow the individual with a certain immunity to tension.

1) Practice optimism.
2) Do one thing at a time.
3) Not to seek to always win.
4) To concern oneself with doing things for others, and to not isolate oneself from others.
5) Do not criticize others; try to understand them.
6) Avoid idleness and daydreaming.
7) Practice patience and tolerance.
8) Practice tidiness.
9) Let off steam.
10) Possess one's own philosophy of life.
11) Possess a sense of humor.
12) Enjoy the simple things of life.

PRACTICE OPTIMISM

The human being's entire life, including all physical events, is based on his habitual thoughts. Negative thoughts seriously disturb the individual's psychic and organic balance while at the same time producing an artificial reaction of stress. The pessimist lives permanently projected into the future in the anticipation of negative experiences. His negativism often prevents him from pursuing certain enterprises in which he might be successful. The pessimist's personal initiative is paralyzed and he adamantly refuses to acknowledge that there is another side to the coin. By adopting an optimistic outlook on life, one cannot ignore the dangers which might arise in one's path, but a person can acknowledge that a positive mental attitude may considerably help him to succeed. The man who succeeds is a "fanatic of optimism" and as such tenaciously refuses to acknowledge the possibility of failure; he will never admit that possibility, although he may fail in certain enterprises. He merely thinks, "I was not successful now, but next time I will be." Positive thoughts definitely influence the maintenance of an adequate psychic equilibrium and also allow for greater intellectual yield. At the same time they are invaluable elements for inducing a state of relaxation.

DO ONE THING AT A TIME

Doing several things simultaneously, hinders thought and influences the nervous system by preventing the individual from living effectively in the present moment. It is said that shyness, for example, is no more than a desire to solve all one's problems simultaneously, which blocks the conscious mind.

It is recommended to always do one thing at a time in order to live every possible moment to the fullest. This is a steadfast guideline that should be applied to all one's actions. Remember that the "I" is the exact point of union between the past and future.

NOT TO SEEK TO ALWAYS WIN

It is absolutely necessary for the individual to know how to lose. This does not refer to "oriental fatalism," but an intelligent acknowledgment that one cannot always win. Any defeat, in whatever field it may have occurred, always offers some profound lesson. A person should always attempt to explain where the fault lay when he fails. The analysis of personal failures will definitely furnish the individual with the necessary tools for victory. Some people funnel all their hopes towards the attainment of a goal they have set for themselves, and when that goal is not fulfilled, they fall apart psychically. The man who knows how to lose is the one who does not waste his time crying over his failures, but who immediately sets himself in motion to try again. Those who ignore the art of losing wisely squander their time and energy in meaningless laments and often set up mental hurdles that prevent them from action.

TO CONCERN ONESELF WITH DOING THINGS FOR OTHERS, AND TO NOT ISOLATE ONESELF FROM OTHERS

The isolated individual feeds on his own thoughts and emotions, shutting out progress and evolution brought about by the interaction with others. The introvert has a very limited mental life, because he does not receive the impact of different ideas or experience the beneficial effects of cultural interchange. The human being needs a social life for his emotional stability. Due to this need he cannot afford to wait for people to come to him; he must take the initiative to seek and go to them. He must break through the selfish circle of his own interest and for a while stop thinking about what benefits him, and concern himself with doing things for others. Concern for the welfare of the community should be part and parcel of any civilized individual, but personal interest often makes one forget the interests of one's collective. Many people who find life tedious and lacking in stimuli can reap adequate compensation by working for the benefit of the community. Of course, this point does not exclusively concern only the community, but also its members in particular.

DO NOT CRITICIZE OTHERS; TRY TO UNDERSTAND THEM

The habit of constantly criticizing people reveals an absorbent and dominant nature that seeks to mold others in one's own way. Criticism is always a wish to change people according to what the individual thinks fitting. This may become a dangerous habit, because in the end it leads the individual to an erroneous appreciation of human beings, since he merely observes their faults and excludes their virtues. Someone said, "I have never encountered a human being who did not surpass me in some way." In other words, there's something to be learned from every person one meets. To not criticize people has a broader significance than it may seem, for at the core it implies "understanding others." Many individuals say that people don't understand them. And why should people bother to understand them particularly? It is far more sensible to think that it is the individual who should bother to understand people, not the reverse.

AVOID IDLENESS AND DAYDREAMING

Idle imaginative wandering causes serious harm to the individual if it becomes a habit, because he becomes accustomed to living in an unreal world created according to his own requirements. This escape from reality slowly undermines one's personal initiative and capacity for adaptation until the individual ends up living in a world of fantasy. As problems of the nervous type are generally caused by an incapacity to face up to reality, one can realize that by eluding reality one is merely deepening the conflict.

PRACTICE PATIENCE AND TOLERANCE

Patience is the chief virtue that facilitates mental concentration. The capacity to become absorbed in the study of or observation of something always demands patient, sustained attention. Impatience, on the contrary, encourages states of nervous tension, because the individual lives projected into the future. The impatient individual is quite incapable of living in the present moment and if he could, he would live out his whole life all at once. Uncertainty about the future, is to a great extent, the cause of this problem because the individual makes constant efforts to foresee the future.

PRACTICE TIDINESS

Tidiness permits greater efficiency at work and greater economy of one's energy. Generally, the physically tidy person is also mentally disciplined. Mental tidiness is indispensable for thinking clearly and increases one's intellectual yield. Besides, the fact of submitting oneself to a discipline, it also offers greater stability. Tidiness is integration; untidiness is disintegration.

LET OFF STEAM

The introvert who never lets off steam is at a considerable disadvantage as opposed to the extrovert. Emotional repression gradually increases emotional and nervous pressure until there is a breakdown. The letting off of steam is the "safety valve" that brings about muscular, mental and emotional relaxation. Nevertheless, it is not advisable to let off steam by giving free rein to one's wrath for example. It is preferable to channel one's tension towards some other constructive activity such as sport, study, or a hobby.

POSSESS ONE'S OWN PHILOSOPHY OF LIFE

When the individual does not possess his own profound philosophy of life, he is constantly exposed to instability and lack of equilibrium. Anybody with strong, profound beliefs is by nature more stable and able to withstand pressing situations unscathed. It is possible for someone to have totally erroneous concepts of many things, but if his ideas are solid from the point of view of personal belief, then he will maintain emotional stability. One's highest achievement lies in the fact that one's ideals be the fruit of deep comprehension before they are incorporated as beliefs.

POSSESS A SENSE OF HUMOR

A lack of a sense of humor often leads one to adopt the attitude of taking life very seriously which takes away some of its appeal. It is advisable to know how to spot and understand the funny side of even difficult situations. One should not take life or oneself too seriously.

ENJOY THE SIMPLE THINGS OF LIFE

People usually live "waiting" for some future event that will enable them to attain the happiness they desire, which invariably prevents them from enjoying what they already have. Thus, the human being has the bad habit of thinking about all that he lacks instead of about what he already has. This prevents him from enjoying what he has already achieved. In its ultimate sense, happiness is only the capacity of a person to live fully in the present moment. Tedium, sadness, and boredom belong to those individuals who do not know how to observe the marvels of the present moment. One must learn to discover the wonderful world of the simple things of life and enjoy them.

These twelve points sum up the attitudes which will help one to lead a more prosperous and healthy existence, and to successfully withstand the ups and downs of life. They are a code for mental health, and nervous and emotional equilibrium.

SUMMARY OF THE METHOD OF HYPSOCONSCIOUSNESS AND INSTRUCTIONS FOR ITS USE

We shall briefly summarize a few ideas that make up the central structure of HypsoConsciousness and which require further emphasis for the student to take better advantage of this method.

The human being has two fundamental states of consciousness: wakefulness and sleep. As there are many degrees of profundity in sleep, there are also many levels of depth in wakefulness. The human being's habitual state is a low level of wakefulness. Similarly, there are also diverse degrees of consciousness. The lowest level is that of deep sleep, and the highest is the result of super-conscious training. Despite being "awake," the individual's psyche usually remains immersed in the oneiric state that interferes with his intellectual functioning, thus preventing an accurate appreciation of reality. Hence, daytime thought is a kind of daydreaming which goes unnoticed by the individual himself. And because the human being's motivation for evolution is inadequate, he remains an intelligent animal, although *hypoconscious* as far as his latent possibilities are concerned. HypsoConsciousness, through its diverse repertoire of exercises attempts to elevate the individual's level of consciousness which enables him to attain self-control, equilibrium, stability, calm and a superior intellectual state. In sum, it introduces the individual to a new, more elevated, more human and true state of consciousness.

In his habitual condition the human being does not really exist as an individual, but rather as an "anti-individual." The "anti-individual" is a man who is incapable of self-determination; he is a mere projection of the social group, without a life of his own. This man has no "I"; he only has a "we." The "I" is that which is the individual's own; the "we" is all that is not his own. The "we" is a structure that has been implanted by force; the "I" is a formation born of one's own determination and fed by conscious reflective learning.

HypsoConsciousness shapes the "I" and leads it

toward its complete maturity. Only the person who has a fully grown, mature and adult "I" can justly say: "I am a human being." This true individual manages to define himself and free himself from the irrational and purely emotional behavior of the mass, so that he attains true fulfillment as a CONSCIOUS AND INTELLIGENT HUMAN INDIVIDUAL.

HOW TO USE THE METHOD OF HYPSOCONSCIOUSNESS CORRECTLY

It is essential to first understand the theoretical aspects of HypsoConsciousness. It must be stressed that there is a great difference between *knowing* and *understanding*. Comprehension is a process of profound understanding that arouses great changes in the structure of the personality because the individual incorporates within himself new ways of adaptation as a result of what he has fully understood. Conscious study makes a person change. It enables him to integrate his personality at higher levels, on the condition that he has properly understood the subject. It is suggested that one studies the theoretical part particularly and in detail before going on to the practical part of the system of HypsoConsciousness. Once understood correctly, it is advisable to begin the actual exercises and follow the order recommended.

To make this easier, all the exercises are listed with their respective numbers:

Exercise No. 1	Complete Breathing
Exercise No. 2	Morning Breathing
Exercise No. 3	Breathing for Relaxation
Exercise No. 4	Imperceptible Breathing
Exercise No. 5	Relaxation and Mastery of the Imagination
Exercise No. 6	Mental Concentration 1
Exercise No. 7	Mental Concentration 2
Exercise No. 8	The Mental Void
Exercise No. 9	Conscious Movements
Exercise No. 10	Voice Consciousness
Exercise No. 11	Consciousness of the "I"
Exercise No. 12	Solving Problems
Exercise No. 13	Applied Use of the Intellect

These diverse exercises may either be applied to specific situations, or for a practical method of a general nature. When used specifically, they bring about a momentary elevation of the level of consciousness that enables one to overcome the problem at hand. Used generally, they tend to elevate the level of consciousness gradually.

As a general guideline, the following order is recommended:

1st month: Exercises No. 1, 2 and 5

Exercise No. 2 should only begin after mastering the technique of No. 1. Exercise No. 5, regarding relaxation of the eyes, should be carried out at least four times a day for periods of no less than two minutes.

2nd month: Exercise No. 2, 3, 5 and 6

3rd month: Exercise No. 2, 3, 5, 7 and 9

4th month: Exercise No. 2, 5, 8 and 9

5th month: Exercise No. 2, 5, 8 and 9

6th month: Exercise No. 2, 5, 9, 10 and 11

7th month: Exercise No. 2, 5, 9, 10 and 11

After the seventh month, one's daily training routine should consist of Exercises No. 2, 3, 5, 9 and 11 as a norm and as the minimum amount recommendable. If time permits, one could also do Exercise No. 8, *the Mental Void*, and if not daily, at least once a week for a period of no less than ten minutes.

If desired, one may practice the other exercises occasionally in order to overcome temporary conflicts.

No rigid norms can be applied as far as practice is concerned for one must use one's own criterion to persevere with the exercises which will bring about the best results. Each person must adjust the length of time, the exercises, and repetitions to his own personal needs.

All the exercises without exception produce an elevation of the level of consciousness although through different mechanisms. Remember that the elevation of the level of consciousness is always synonymous with relaxation, calm, mental clarity, self-determination, energy, and higher intelligence. All the exercises produce relaxation and harmonize psychic and physical unity so that they permit optimum yield and the possibility for the individual to fulfill himself and attain true happiness.

CONCLUDING REMARKS

The central subject of this work is consciousness, the fundamental nature of one's psychic life. The meaning given to the word "consciousness" does not concern a knowledge of good and evil and differs from the psychological counterpart. Here, "to be conscious," means to have a high level of consciousness.

There are many degrees of consciousness, ranging from deep sleep to extreme awakeness. Unconsciousness or consciousness do not exist, only a high or low level of consciousness. A high level of consciousness can be considered synonymous with being awake. Yet the problem is not quite as simple as that, because the intention of HypsoConsciousness is to exalt consciousness as the human being's maximum quality, as precisely the determining factor of his human quality that essentially differentiates him from animals. Therefore, the above definition is not sufficient, since many animals are normally more awake than human beings and therefore appear to be more conscious than humans. We need to draw a line between the meaning of a "high state of wakefulness" and a "high level of consciousness." The difference between them was not taken into account before in order to facilitate the understanding of the mechanisms which are in themselves highly complex.

"A high level of wakefulness" means to be wide awake, far more than usual. "A high level of consciousness" means having attained the shaping of an adult, mature and considerably developed "I." The case for example, of a wide-awake idiot might arise, but it would be impossible for an individual with a "high level of consciousness," not to be intelligent and wide-awake. The aim is to give the human being a new psychological dimension, based upon the most significant fact of his psychic existence, that is, the phenomenon of being only half-awake. Sometimes it may be necessary to forget for a moment those complicated and obsolete theories that focus on the problem of the individual but which never touch the question: "What is the individual?" nor penetrate into his nucleus, that is into his "I," the necessary and unmovable foundation of his human status.

A new meaning must be given to the word "intelligence," that can encompass and describe more profoundly and accurately, this precious faculty. In the strictest sense, only those who possess a high level of consciousness can be called "humanly intelligent." Man's intelligence is relative and variable if he does not have a mature "I." Actually, consciousness is the only truly human quality that the animal totally lacks. The more conscious an individual is (that is, the higher his level of consciousness), the farther removed he will be from the animal; the less conscious he is, the closer he is to the animal. Thus, a man may be highly intelligent (in its common sense), but not particularly human, that is, not highly conscious.

In order to obtain a high level of consciousness it is necessary to first attain an elevated state of awakeness because this enables one to expel the oneiric condition from one's psyche and thus carry out conscious reflective learning which is what builds the "I." The highly intelligent, but oneirically influenced person, never attains a high level of consciousness, unless he first manages to fully awaken. This awakening involves serious difficulties, for man's common faculties do not help him in this endeavor. He must on the other hand, resort to fortifying that small part of himself that is overwhelmed by the oneiric web of his psychological "I." If this "I" is too small or weak, which depends on countless circumstances that we shall not mention here, it is not possible for the individual to ever manage to rid himself of sleep, unless he makes considerable effort to do so.

HypsoConsciousness exercises are designed to encourage the individual's wakefulness and the subsequent development of his "I."

We must stress the difficulties in understanding involved in the problem of consciousness and the "I," for in order to penetrate its profound meaning one must have a minimum level of consciousness. People usually lack this, however cultured and intelligent they may appear to be. The phenomena related to consciousness are only accessible to one's own experience and the individual must first attain a higher state of wakefulness if he is to analyze and study them carefully. One cannot demand great comprehension from somebody who has not rid himself of his oneiric condition. Thus, tangible proof of the high level of consciousness can only be acquired through direct experience.

It is essential to understand that the acquisition of a high degree of consciousness is an unavoidable duty of the human being, for it is the maximum attribute of his human condition. The fact of being human involves shouldering certain unavoidable responsibilities, for to shirk them means to a certain extent losing one's humanness. This is without a doubt the task of consciousness.

Many people are content to be merely intelligent animals and do not mind living unconsciously and ignorantly regarding the meaning of their lives. Yet any individual capable of thinking objectively and properly will acknowledge how important it is for man to become more human.

Unfortunately, social organization openly conspires to keep the individual restricted to the state of sleep. Nowadays, throughout the world, that which encourages sleep is exalted and that which brings about wakefulness is reproached. We are a race of sleeping gods who behave like animals.

At the expense of his consciousness, the human organism possesses many natural mechanisms that demand fulfillment. All that encages man within rigid dogmas is hypnotic. Non-digested studies or badly planned ones, the countless religious and political creeds, the excess of consumer culture, the bombardment of advertising and analytical superficiality, all limit the possibilities of the mind, stratifying creative intelligence and driving the individual to unconscious behavior.

A university student would not for one instant dare to question what was being taught by his professors, nor to doubt its value. This is deplorable because all true knowledge begins with doubt. The student generally restricts himself to learning concepts by memory, rather than truly comprehending them. Moreover, his state of suggestibility in relation to his teachers is so strong that he often tacitly accepts their personal ideas and ways. Most professionals usually leave the university turned into "stereotypes" within their specialty, with similar minds and personalities, unless they previously had a true understanding of their acquired knowledge. Really, knowledge without understanding is mere dead weight and an obstacle to shaping the higher "I" that is truly stable and mature.

Any integrated group, or psychological mass can annul rational individual conduct in its members by substituting it with a purely emotional and impulsive behavior. Logic, reason and good judgment can be easily replaced by fanaticism, prejudice, superstition and external influences.

The individual in isolation is often exposed to irrational behavior, driven by the pride of a weak, unreflective and unconscious "I." Pride and vanity thus limit the intelligence by placing the individual in a selfish position.

The young rebel unconsciously seeks his liberation from the mass by existing as an individual, but unfortunately, he does not do this in an intelligent way. Hence, he adopts an attitude of opposition to pre-established habits and norms, so that to a certain extent he manages to assert his individuality in a world of "anti-individuals." What other defense is left to him? What else can a person do to avoid disappearing, to being absorbed by the vortex of the social being? It is possible that the youngster who fights against the current is more awake than others with traditional ideas, because at least he realizes the need to assert his individuality.

The hopeless individual is the one who, although he is asleep, feels happy and refuses to accept the mere possibility of an unknown state of wakefulness. Unfortunately, there are many people of this type; their minds tightly shut to all that threatens to disturb their profound sleep. Of course, nobody likes being suddenly awakened and obliged to meditate. The mass instinctively reacts against all that implies the effort of reflective intellectual elaboration and it prefers to take on the prefabricated behavior of its leaders.

The history of mankind is full of examples of the bitter struggle between obscurantism and knowledge. Fanaticism and intolerance have been, are, and always will be the worst enemies of human progress. However, there have been individuals in all ages with alert minds who have aspired to a greater comprehension of themselves and who, guided by this ideal, have managed to become true human, conscious and intelligent individuals.

ABOUT THE AUTHOR

John Baines, founder and director of the John Baines Institute, is a contemporary philosopher with a growing popularity in the United States and over 1,000,000 books sold worldwide. He is dedicated to teaching the human being how to raise his level of awareness through the practice of special techniques and studies. This latest title of Mr. Baines, *HypsoConsciousness,* is a collection of these techniques and serves as a guidebook to obtaining a higher level of awareness, to achieving personal success and freedom from exaggerated states of nervous tension that plague contemporary man. *HypsoConsciousness,* is in fact a unique term coined by Mr. Baines to describe the state of heightened awareness achieved through bringing mind and body together in the present moment.

As a man he encompasses the universal qualities of true humanness by actively promoting individual development. His unique perspective, common to all his books, in particular to *The Secret Science, The Stellar Man , The Science of Love,* and now *HypsoConsciousness,* unites contemporary psychological practice with philosophical wisdom in a tangible and operative manner. All his works are intended to enrich and harmonize man's understanding of himself and his relation to all.

Further information regarding the Teachings of John Baines can be obtained by contacting the New York Headquarters of the John Baines Institute at the address below:

USA
The John Baines Institute, Inc.
P.O. Box 8556
FDR Station
New York, NY 10150, U.S.A.

The John Baines Institute also offers instruction worldwide in the following countries:

AUSTRALIA
ARGENTINA
BULGARIA
CHILE
RUSSIA
SPAIN
VENEZUELA

Other books by John Baines can be ordered through the publisher or faxed to (212) 249-7028.

☐ **The Secret Science**
   ISBN 1-882692-01-2   @ $7.95

☐ **The Stellar Man**
   ISBN 0-87542-026-5   @ $9.95

☐ **The Science of Love**
   ISBN 1-882692-00-4   @ $12.95

☐ **HypsoConsciousness**
   ISBN 1-882692-02-0   @ $9.95

Books are also available in Spanish, Bulgarian, Russian, Italian and Portuguese.

Use this page for ordering:

THE JOHN BAINES COLLECTION
P.O. Box 8556, F.D.R. Station
NYC, NY 10150

Please send me the above title(s). I am enclosing $ ——————
(Please add $3.00 per order to cover shipping and handling). Send check or money order—no cash or C.O.D.s please. New York Residents must add 8.25% tax.

Mr./Mrs./Ms.————————————————————

Address————————————————————————

City/State/Zip—————————————————————

Prices and availability subject to change without notice.

Fold Over

Fold this sheet of paper as shown below.
Reinforce it with some cardboard.